Twice Broke *But* Never Broken

Richard L. Freitag

Twice Broke But Never Broken
Copyright © 2021 by Richard L. Freitag

Library of Congress Control Number: 2021910869
ISBN-13: Paperback: 978-1-64749-482-7
ePub: 978-1-64749-483-4

All rights reserved. No part of this publication may be reproduced, distributed, or transmitted in any form or by any means, including photocopying, recording, or other electronic or mechanical methods, without the prior written permission of the publisher or author, except in the case of brief quotations embodied in critical reviews and certain other noncommercial uses permitted by copyright law.

Although every precaution has been taken to verify the accuracy of the information contained herein, the author and publisher assume no responsibility for any errors or omissions.No liability is assumed for damages that may result from the use of information contained within.

Printed in the United States of America

GoToPublish LLC
1-888-337-1724
www.gotopublish.com
info@gotopublish.com

CONTENTS

Preface v
Introduction vii
Part I – Family History 1
   Ancestry and "Pop's" Story 3
   Brothers in Business 17
   Partnership No More! 27
Part II – Family Business 31
   Sole Proprietorship 33
   Kenny's Dream Job 43
   Different Direction 59
Part III - New Leadership and New Direction 77
   Downturn with a Safety Net 79
   Early Successes 83
   My Dream Job 103
Part IV - Broke! 113
   Harsh Realities 115
   Facing Others 119
   Shattered Self 125

Part V – A Break from Broke 127
   Intermission Mission 129
   Planning the Way Out.. 137
   Salvation Sale 141

Part VI - Mid-Life Do-Over **147**
   Back in the Game 149
   Wannabees Attack 155
   Exit – My Way 169

Part VII – Reflections..**173**
   The Portly Gladiator 175
   What Once Was.. 179
   Turned Down for Loan?... 181
   Whirling 185
   Really, "Red"? 187
   Those Guys 191
   Guaranteed 193
   The Trabant 195
   Contractor/Philosopher 199
   Nuts and Bolts 203
   A Few Random Thoughts..................................... 209
   Afterthoughts... 213

PREFACE

There is a rollercoaster ride known as American entrepreneurship. It is a ride not everyone has the guts to attempt. It takes courage and stamina to endure the upsides and the downsides of small business in our uniquely American free enterprise system. If you have not been made aware of this by now, being involved in private business, though exhilarating, can be a most brutal ride.

My story begins four generations back with poor European peasants emigrating to America. In their struggle to carve out an existence, they attempted all sorts of private enterprise. These are stories of perseverance and that "never give up" attitude, often involving extreme risk-taking. Among them are stories of success and failure and success again – sometimes surviving the rise and fall of the cyclical nature of business, but sometimes not.

Using my own experience as an entrepreneur, I hope to show you the joys of operating a small business as well as the harsh realities and hardship of "going it alone" and suffering financial setbacks. As I tell my stories, I am also going to tell you what I think about our free enterprise system, including my answers to questions like;

- How does a small businessperson handle a financial setback?
- Suffered a setback? What steps are needed to "get back in the game"?

- How to deal with bankers and creditors to win.
- Lessons to be learned by those who need to find direction.
- Thoughts, ideas and reflections on this uniquely American experience.

These are stories of independent, freedom loving business people who had the courage to hang on despite setbacks.

Enjoy a glimpse into the world of our distinctive American free enterprise business experience. This is Americana - American business human-interest stories. All of this is shared with you by a veteran of 40 years of the American small business experience in the United States.

Enjoy the ride.

INTRODUCTION

My right arm had quit functioning normally. Medical examinations, tests, MRI's and analysis by several specialists determined that I had a bone growth in the interior of the vertebra in the neck region of my upper spine. This was pinching off the spinal cord nerves in that area of my spine causing arm immobility problems. Spinal surgery at Mayo Clinic in Rochester, Minnesota, was going to have to happen to fix my problem.

The surgeon told me, "It is my duty to inform you that there is a one in two hundred chance that you will wake up from this procedure paralyzed from the neck down. We are dealing with some *very expensive real estate*", as he put it, "when we work in that area of the spine." My surgeon was sort of a wise guy. When he spoke, he had this genuine self-confidence, call it a swagger, a certain bravado about him– not arrogance, really – but just a sort of "moxie" or "attitude". I appreciated that. I especially appreciated that he had this sort confidence when it was *my* "very expensive real estate" that he was going to be working on. I believe you've just got to have huge self-confidence to be a neuro-surgeon, but better yet, to work in that area of the upper spine with all the nerves and muscles and the spinal cord. Hit the spinal cord and it's all over. Besides this "attitude" thing, neuro-surgeons on his level need plenty of skill and a whole lot of guts to do what they do for a living.

So, I asked him, "So how many of these have you done? In other words, I might be a bit more nervous if you've completed 199 of these procedures without problems and now, here I am at number 200." I had to do my own version of the wise guy thing right back at him. He chuckled.

Naturally, I did not sleep well that night before the surgery. I only remember that the day of my surgery started out real early in the morning. All the prep work, etc., etc. At last, I was "put under."

The next thing I knew, there is an eerie light of which I am aware… almost. It comes from a doorway which has clouded, foggy edges. I seem to be in a semi-conscious daze. I am very sleepy. There is a terrible stabbing pain in the neck area of my upper spine. Try to focus. My vision is blurred, strange. Everything I view is hazy – surrounded by this clouded gray frame. There are no real corners in this room. Hospital room? Yes, that's it. Though I can't see her, my wife is there at my side and I know she is speaking to me but I cannot understand a thing that she is saying. Then, black out.

Again, this semi-awareness. That piercing, horrible pain is there. Yes, definitely hospital room. My wife is speaking to me again but I still do not understand what she is saying. Out, yet another time.

Return to near consciousness. A voice – not my wife's – butts into whatever my wife was saying. Must be a nurse, I'm not sure. In a very loud voice, this person (this nurse?) questions, "Richard, do you know where you are?"

"Yes, I am at the Mayo Clinic's St. Mary's Hospital in Rochester, Minnesota."

"Very good", says the voice. "Now, do you know who the president of the United States is?"

"No! And neither do you.", I replied. Laughter, then I faded out yet again.

It is early December 2000. The outcome of the recent presidential election has not yet been determined between Al Gore and George W. Bush. Election officials are still counting ballots and "chards" in Florida to determine a winner. That's why I answered the nurse the way I did when she asked me who the president was, I told her I didn't know and neither did she.

Consciousness has returned one more time. The consciousness this time makes me very cognizant of the pain in the neck region of my upper spine. This time I can clearly hear when my wife speaks to me to tell me that the nurse will be back soon to give me a shot for the pain. This time I understand what she is saying. Whatever the shot is going to be, I know I need the stuff because the pain is intense.

My surroundings are clear now – no more haze. Yes, I am very aware of my presence in a hospital room. I look up at the television. I can see it clearly. The news media is all caught up in the recent presidential election results and the confusion surrounding the event is making this the current hot news topic. My physical pain is so intense that I really do not care at all what program is tuned in for my viewing pleasure.

Wait a minute. I have a real need to check certain things out. After all, the surgeon told me prior to the operation that there was a one in two hundred chance that I would wake up after surgery paralyzed from the neck down. Well, let's check things out.

Right arm moves a little bit but not really right yet – check. Right hand and fingers move – check. Left arm moves and left hand and fingers move – check. Right leg moves – check. Right foot and leg move and right toes wiggle – check. Left foot and left leg move - left toes wiggle – check. The operation must have been a success as far as I can determine at this point. What a relief! I am not paralyzed!

The nurse has returned to the room and asks me to repeat what I have just done myself so that she can see if there is movement in my appendages. As she puts me through this drill, she has injected some pain-relieving drugs into my intravenous contraption. The drugs take affect quickly, the intensity of the pain subsides and I become very mellow fading once again into the realm of semi-consciousness.

As I awaken once again, the pain in my upper spine is at a much lower level than before the drugs – rating the pain at four on a scale of one to ten. Yes, I am "drugged up." But I do feel fully coherent now. As such, I am fully aware of another pain which has been affecting me psychologically, emotionally and, in a certain way, physiologically for some time now which even spinal surgery can not cure. I am back to facing the reality that while recovering from surgery, I have another problem to face which I will not be able to recover from quite so quickly. My business is broke. I've nearly "lost it all".

As I spent the next couple of months recovering from my spinal surgery, I kept thinking back to this past business season and what had all gone wrong. How could things get this bad in such a short time? How could a season which started with such promise turn into such a nightmare? How could a comfortable financial position at the beginning of the season collapse in such a hurry? Presently I have a debt load which I cannot repay because I cannot collect what I'm due on either of the project contract balances. I had two contracts going this past season. In one case, the worst case, the income will not even begin to cover the costs associated with the project. To put things in business language, my finances are "upside down".

As of now, lawyers will most likely determine the final outcomes of both contracts. From past experience, the only thing I am absolutely certain of is that when lawyers get involved, I will lose. The question remaining is how bad will the damages end up being?

In a rather strange sense, there is some good news, if it can be called that. I know exactly what to do in this present predicament for myself and my company. You see, I have experience. The reason I have this knowledge and experience is that this is the *second* time in my life that I have gone broke. Having suffered this experience previously, I know that the real problem is not my company's financial situation. Far more important are the personal issues I must deal with to overcome the shattering effects of yet another business failure.

Admittedly, writing about going broke in business would not be quite so terrible except that the stories I am about to relate are my own. Financial loss – going broke – is a fact of life in the real world of business and the free enterprise system. Individuals and businesses go broke every day. To belabor specific statistical information on business failures seems redundant. You can find this information at any library if interested.

Given the statistics on business failure, it's hard to believe that people continue to give free enterprise a try. And, yet they do. Had these brave souls studied the information on the subject, they'd be aware that their chances of survival in private enterprise are poor at best. The odds are stacked against them. And still, they continue to try. These courageous entrepreneurs remain steadfastly unfazed by the possibility of failure. It takes a lot of guts to be self-employed and do what businesspeople do.

Any number of history's great free market entrepreneurial success stories began with failure or even multiple failures. You would recognize names of some of these giants of industry who have suffered financial setback or gone broke. The difference between these greats and others who have suffered financial setbacks is that these people never gave up. That is to say, *even though broke, they were never broken.*

Based on many of America's great success stories of the past, I believe that somehow, someway, there has to be something good, something worthwhile, something of a positive nature in going broke. Reviewing what went wrong, learning the lessons from this most negative experience and then moving on is absolutely necessary for anyone who has suffered a business setback. It is in this searching for positives, I have discovered, that makes it possible to rise above any mere temporary financial predicament. Going broke will be the final chapter, if and only if, we are willing to accept the premise of the finality of it all. This acceptance, constitutes a much deeper level of failure than the mere financial failure of the business itself. Rather than merely a business issue, it becomes a personal issue.

As I will point out, the much larger problems are that of the personal shattered self-image and the inner, personal feelings of failure. These forces create wonderful excuses to simply quit – to give up – to never try again. However, going broke, suffering a financial setback, is not and cannot be viewed as THE END. Going broke is really nothing more than a harsh form of character development and a teaching/learning tool for those who wish to stay in business.

My past experiences have taught me that business setbacks are nothing more than a part of the business continuum. There are no guarantees in business. while there are "ups" in business, there are certainly "downs" as well. This is reality, and to be in business, one must be able to deal in that sort of harsh reality on a daily basis.

The goal of this book is threefold;

1. It is my hope that the stories and the thoughts I share will be of a constructive nature to give help, hope and maybe even inspiration to others who may have suffered through a business downturn. Independent business owners who have suffered a business failure need to know that being broke financially does not necessarily equate with being a broken human being.

2. It is my desire that these stories be lessons in perseverance. Those who read this need to know that you may be broke financially - that can be fixed. You need to know that being a broken human being is a tougher fix. What you need to know is that you will stay broken only as long as you lack the desire to try again. If you choose to continue to make excuses based on self-pity, you will not, you cannot get back in the game.

3. On a personal level, writing this book is a therapeutic way for me to get this debacle out of my system and off my mind. This financial tragedy that has happened to me for a second time in my business career must be dealt with. This "getting it out" is, more or less, a cleansing of my mind which has been tormented by my latest, as with my first, business failure.

If you should find some encouragement or direction or worthwhile thoughts to ponder as a result of reading this book, I will feel this writing exercise will have well been worth the effort.

PART I – FAMILY HISTORY
There is a Pattern

ANCESTRY AND "POP'S" STORY

Being a self-employed independent businessman has always been a source of pride for me. Tracing my family lineage, I find that my family surname may well carry some sort of human genetic mutation. You see, I am the descendent of a long line, I mean a very, very long line of self-employed, independent business people. My family is Germanic Swiss and comes from the village of Elm, Canton (similar to our state) Glarus, Switzerland. My family name is Germanic for the day of the week – Friday – in direct translation from the German to the English Language. My family's history is traced back to 1289 A.D. in a 483-page book by Frederick and Alice Zweifel of Belleville, Wisconsin. This family history is unique in that not only is the "who begot who" of the blood line recorded, but the occupations of the various ancestors are listed in the book as well. Following the lineage and the occupations way back, Freitag's were primarily farmers, but also traders, craftsmen, merchants or artisans. But they were always independent, risk-taking entrepreneurs.

Family histories, no matter how detailed, can furnish only limited information; i.e; dates of birth, names, dates marriages, children, dates of death, etc. Even given the occupational information in this detailed history of my family, I find that the missing information about the personalities of those who have gone before me could really add color and give more meaning to an otherwise basically boring chronology. Were there only a way to recreate these missing personalities.

This is the real human-interest portion of the family history which could certainly add a great deal of substance to the past that we can never know. Only the fading memories of our elderly relatives and a few other folks who knew family members can carry us back in time.

My search into my ancestry, besides the Zweifel book, is based on long conversations and extensive note-taking with two elderly aunts, my mother, my late uncle and my late father and the bookkeeper who ran the office when my father and my uncle were business partners. These treasured times spent together talking over "the good old days" and the stories that were shared with me have given me a glimpse into the seven hundred year plus history of my paternal family. These conversations have allowed me to "get to know" the personalities of some of the more recent members of the family of whom I knew little.

Although I am aware of certain facts of my family's history, I never really gave a great deal of thought to the repeating theme in this family history. I really never came face-to-face with a recurring fact throughout this long and storied family's history. Interestingly, as I am about to share, I am not the first family member to suffer financial setbacks. Not only am I *not* the first – as a matter of fact – I am merely the most recent member in my long family lineage to go broke!

Johan Jacob Freitag was my paternal great grandfather. In 1845, Johan emigrated from the Village of Elm (now a district or suburb of the City of Glarus), Canton Glarus, Switzerland, to the United States of America. It was in Glarus that his ancestors had made their home for nearly six hundred years.

The Swiss are meticulous record keepers. Being that this is the story of Swiss emigrants, I have not only the name of the ship and the date Johan and his family sailed from LeHavre, France, but also the name the Great Lakes vessel and the date they sailed from the state of New York to Milwaukee, in the territory (3 years prior to statehood) of Wisconsin. From Milwaukee, Johan moved his family to Wisconsin's Swiss settlement in Green County (south-central), where he was a dairy farmer. Johan and his wife Maria had ten children, one of which, Edward Johan, was my grandfather.

My grandfather, Edward Johan Freitag, I knew only as "Pop" when I was a small child. I remember only two things specifically about him. He would always dig out his coin purse and hand his grandchildren a shiny dime and he enjoyed eating popcorn but only the white kernel stuff. Other than that, the truth is, I really never got to know my grandfather at all. He died when I was only nine years old. Any information I have about Pop was shared with me by others. Although my dad, my uncle and my aunt never said so in so many words, Pop had to have been a real wild man in his younger days.

How very interesting it would have been to have had the opportunity to talk to Pop on a man-to-man basis. I'm certain the stories would have been a lot more fun, more colorful and a whole lot more interesting. I'm convinced that this history would have come alive had I had direct delivery of the episodes from the man who actually lived the experiences. Unfortunately, this option was never really possible because of my age at the time of his death.

Pop was born May 10,1882 on the dairy farm outside of Monticello, Wisconsin. Since he was not the firstborn son in this Swiss family, he knew he would inherit nothing. In the time tested, long-standing Swiss family tradition of birthright, everything was inherited by the first-born son. Children born after the firstborn son inherited nothing. So, Pop knew he would have to make his own way in the world without any help of any kind from his family.

Pop moved off the family farm in his teens so as not to interfere with his eldest brothers farming operations. Once off the family farm, he drifted for a time taking odd jobs all related to his farming background. These various jobs offered poor pay and few challenges for a young man looking for excitement. He was never an employee of anyone's for too long. He had a need to be independent, free, on his own.

Cattle dealing was Pop's first endeavor as a young businessman. Horse and cattle buying, selling, swapping, trading and bargaining took place in the area saloons. At that time, saloons were gambling houses as well as bars and sandwich shops. Gambling, apparently, supplemented his income during these early years prior to marriage, I'm told.

In 1906, Pop was married to the daughter of a fairly well-to-do local Swiss immigrant dairy farmer. Grandmother saw to it that she and Pop would be dairy farmers as well. (it sounds like she "wore the pants", so to speak). Afterall, both her parents and his parents had prospered in the dairy farming business. Therefore, the young couple rented a farm, planted crops and milked cows. So, for Pop, it was back to farming.

Gone were his wilder days of horse trading, gambling and the saloon lifestyle. Reverting back to a farmer's lifestyle "throttled back" the rather carefree, even sometimes flamboyant lifestyle of a horse-trader/gambler to which he had become accustomed. Grandmother put an end to card playing, drinking, gambling and horse trading even going so far as to ban playing cards from the home entirely.

He must have been bored out of his mind. Crops and field work and cows, those four-legged milk manufacturing factories that had to be milked twice a day lacked the excitement he craved. The repetitive nature of the dairy farming life, the day-to-day routine were just simply too boring for his appetite. No more wild poker games or the bantering of a good heated horse-trading deal. Dairy farming was just too mundane. He needed a challenge, risk and excitement. When he saw his opportunity, he seized the moment.

Risking everything, Pop ventured into a unique business. Whatever their total net worth in 1908, he pledged it all and borrowed everything he could and placed the entire sum on one grand, gigantic bet – in a business sense that is. He purchased the biggest and best well drilling machine available at the time. Making an investment of this size was not unlike betting the entire pot on one hand of cards in a poker game. He felt alive again. Now he had his challenge. Once again, he had that element of danger. He had the do-or-die, make-or-break risk he craved.

No longer just a dirt farmer on a rented farm, now he was a real businessman in a very high-profile business at that. His entrepreneurial venture was unique to that area of Wisconsin at the time. He had no local competition. He had found this niche – this angle – his own little corner in an exclusive market.

Farmers would stop their field work and townspeople would quit whatever they were doing, I'm told, when Pop moved his machinery from job to job. This gazing, this jaw-dropping, as he passed by these onlookers with the beautiful team of horses and his machinery would swell him with pride. He had elevated himself above his former station in life by taking this risk and he was thoroughly enjoying the rewards of his gamble. In truth, not only was he involved in a unique business, he was "showing off" because of his overblown pride and attention seeking.

Although continuing to do farm work at the end of a day of well drilling to placate Grandmother, this new well drilling business was his passion. He became a well driller of sound reputation. He enjoyed a great deal of business success throughout southern Wisconsin. So successful in fact, that within three years the well drilling machinery was completely paid for. The debt was liquidated and there was money in the bank. The great risk and the early struggles associated with a start-up small business had all been worth the gamble. Life was good! All was well with the young couple except life became too routine for Pop. Without the challenge of big risks and huge debt, things became too mundane and boring. He lacked that do or die risk-taking he craved.

Late in 1911, Pop saw what he considered to be the ultimate opportunity of a lifetime. The government of The United States of America had opened up areas of Montana to the Homestead Act. FREE LAND! This was an opportunity to have a farm of their own for free – no more rent to pay. Better yet, this free land was virgin prairie land – wheat land – and wheat prices were at an all time high. All homesteaders had to do to get in on this deal of a lifetime was to build a house on the property, fence he boundaries, work and occupy the land for a few years and 160 acres of land was your – FREE! Pop saw this as his golden opportunity. Grandmother, of course, did not share his enthusiasm for what she considered a totally unconventional, even foolhardy idea.

Undaunted, Pop knew that if he could convince her to move to Montana. They would become rich beyond their dreams. There were so many positives to support his idea. But it was a "hard sell" to convince his wife to leave the area of their birth as well as leaving area family and friends.

It was no secret in the farming community that wheat prices were at an all-time high. Cash cropping wheat was creating a great deal of wealth as close as the prairie lands of west-central Wisconsin. Large scale wheat farming was going on in western states such as the Dakotas, Kansas, Nebraska and Montana. While very aware of this fact that fortunes were being made in wheat farming, grandmother remained unimpressed with the idea.

He tried another angle. They had their dairy cattle. They could move their dairy cattle out west. Area cash croppers would need milk and those milk sales would supply them with a steady income until the first wheat crop was harvested. This dairying income would afford them a great advantage over all the other homesteaders.

There were other advantages the Freitag's would have over their fellow western adventurers. Pop knew horse-trading and livestock dealing. Then too, there was the advantage of their debt-free financial position. Everything was paid for and there was a small cash reserve in the bank, not huge by any means, but a reserve.

But his clincher, his grand finale, his best ever positive argument for the move west was the well drilling machine. Every homesteader would need a well and Pop would be the only well driller in the area. Everything fit so perfectly. Surely grandmother had to see the promise in his plan. She was not buying into the wisdom of this homesteading idea at all.

How did Pop finally convince her to go? Who knows? Whatever it took, he ultimately got the job done and she agreed to go.

They loaded all of their possessions – farm machinery, cattle, horses, wagons, furniture, etc. in a boxcar and loaded the well drilling machine on a flatcar. They took seating in a coach car for the long trip west by rail. They traveled over a thousand miles to Forsyth, Montana, the County Seat in Rosebud County. From there, it was a twenty-mile trip northwest to Vananda, Montana, which would now be their new home. At Forsyth, they offloaded their possessions from the train, loaded up the horse drawn wagon and headed off to "stake their claim". Once in Vananda, the Freitag's registered with the government office, got directions to their allotted homestead property, headed east of town up and over the rolling grassy knolls. There they found their little piece of paradise and began their adventure.

Pop knew Vananda was the perfect place to locate as soon as they arrived in town. How? The need for water. If you wanted water in Vananda, you had to purchase it. Enterprising teamsters were in the business of hauling water from Frosyth, which was twenty miles away, in horse drawn water tankers. This transported water cost plenty and the Vananda homesteaders had three choices; 1.) pay the price, 2.) go get your own water or, 3.) go without.

If this was not the land of opportunity, the promised land for Pop, the promised land never existed. Just twenty miles from where this expensive water was coming from, sat the only well drilling rig in the territory. And it belonged to Pop. As he saw it, he was in the right place at the right time with the right machine. Ready, set, go. It was time to start making money.

First things first, however. As homesteaders, you had to build a home on your claim. Like all the neighbors, the Freitag's built a sod dugout home with one window and one door. Both of these items had to be purchased at the lumberyard in Forsyth, but the sod bricks were free for the digging. A number of trips had to be made back and forth to Forsyth just to move their possessions from the railroad warehouse to their property. Pop got all the moving done while Grandmother was getting her new sod home, complete with a dirt floor, in order. To appease Grandmother and to convince her that he really was interested in the farming part of the adventure, he left the well drilling machine in Forsyth for the time being.

Besides fencing the property, there were a great many other things to be done around the farm. Fields had to be plowed and harrowed. Wheat had to be planted. A building had to be constructed to house the dairy cattle, horses and farm implements. Not having moved the well drilling machine to Vananda actually served as an incentive for him to work harder and work more quickly. Only when all was in order, could he could finally concentrate his energies on his work of choice, his passion – well drilling.

Now, at last, the time had come to move the well drilling machine from Forsyth to Vananda. This would be the triumphant last move to make ~~from Forsyth~~ and he savored the thought of this trip. Always the shrewd promoter, he did not take the machine directly to their property. Instead, he parked the rig in downtown Vananda for a few days just to allow the interest and curiosity of his fellow homesteaders to reach a fevered pitch. Then he would secure a list of customers certain to be interested in having their own source of water.

When he thought the interest had reached a high point, he took his machine to the Freitag homestead to drill the first well in the Vananda area. Why not drill the first well at the areas only well drillers place? After that initial well, he could only imagine how the customers list would swell. Let the water and the money begin to flow!

He set up his well drilling machine next to the sod house so that the well would be close by and therefore the trip to the well would be less miserable in the cold winter months on the Montana prairie. There he began to drill.

He drilled to the depth where water was usually found back in Wisconsin. But the water was a lot deeper in Montana. He had more or less figured this would be the case. So, he needed to drill deeper. There was, however, another problem, a fact that Pop was *not* prepared to deal with – a fact of nature from which there was no escape. When he did finally hit water at a depth of about 200 feet, the water was *alkaline,* a major problem – a fact of nature from which there was no escape. Alkaline water is non-potable. That is to say, it is not suitable for drinking for either man nor beast. Alkaline water is a salty mineral water which is completely unpalatable.

OK, so abandon that hole and try again. Never one to give up, he moved his rig to a hill east of the house and drilled again. Same result. He hit the water vein, but again it was alkaline. He moved his rig again, this time to the south of the house. Same result again. All of his efforts yielded the same results – water at 200 feet – all alkaline water. Convinced that there had to be good water someplace on the property, he continued to move and drill, move and drill, move and drill. The property had a lot of drilled holes but never one that produced potable water.

How embarrassing. How very humiliating it had to have been for the area's only well driller to have to purchase potable water from the teamsters with the tanker wagons hauling water from Forsyth.

Frustrated, he contracted with the City of Vananda to drill a municipal well for the growing community. Naturally, potable water was a condition of the contract. Like at his own homestead, Pop drilled a lot of holes but none would produce drinkable water.

As their first year of homesteading drew to a close, there was one bright spot to look back on. High prices were paid for a bumper crop wheat harvest. The final standing at the end of year one--Grandmother was a delighted cash cropper while her husband was a disgusted well driller.

Year number two was a repeat of the first.

Year three brought an unexpected surprise. Grandmother was having stomach disorders which required hospitalization. In those times, the closest hospital was located in Dickenson, North Dakota. In late April of 1913, Grandmother was headed east on the train out of Forsyth. Pop hitched the team of horses to the well drilling rig. He followed overland in hopes of success drilling in the Dickenson area while his wife was hospitalized. Grandmothers stomach problem was remedied on May 4, 1913, when she gave birth to their first child, a son, my uncle Edward H. Freitag.

Unlike today, back then women were hospitalized for some time after giving birth. During her extended recovery, Pop was very successfully drilling wells in and around the Dickenson area. Well drilling paid for all the medical and hospital costs as well as yielding a profit. At the time, a wise option may have been to stay in the Dickenson area, but the homestead, the free land was in Vananda so they headed back to Montana with their newborn son and the cash from the well drilling successes in North Dakota.

Back in Vananda, both the wheat cash cropping business and the homesteaders directly tied to the wheat crop were experiencing hard times. A severe drought had caused substantial wheat crop failure in all of eastern Montana that season. The homesteaders were losing financially. Worse yet, most of these folks were in rather precarious financial positions when they embarked on this homesteading adventure. So, even the slightest hiccup in the weather, in crop yield or physical health and/or a variety of other factors would instantly spell financial ruin for many. A number of neighbors had already given up. They left town, left their dreams, gave up their claims and moved on with their lives. Not so the Freitag's. They would "tough it out", try again, not quit and not give up. In an attempt to recover their losses from the crop failure, Pop had to travel farther and farther looking for well drilling work.

The Vananda area's population was depleted due to the drought. Being financially unable to purchase foodstuffs, those hearty soles who remained were subsisting on a diet of wild game, prairie hens, mainly. And all of those who remained, even the local well driller, were still purchasing their drinking water from the teamsters.

Spring came none too early in 1914. With the warm weather, came the renewed hope for a better season of wheat production. As a result of the recent war in Europe coupled with low wheat reserves due to last year's poor harvest on a nation-wide basis, wheat prices were at a record high. The Vananda area survivors got their field work done and the new wheat crop planted as quickly as possible that spring. Spirits ran high as the welcomed rains watered the fields at just the right times. The wheat crop sprouted and hopes rose in anticipation of a super yield. The sun shined, the crop ripened and Pop literally walked through the "amber waves of grain" just a few days prior to the harvest, confident of recouping his losses and once again putting money in the bank.

A new form of disaster struck.

This time a hail storm, combined with high winds, completely flattened the entire wheat crop in the Vananda area. Only an unharvestable two-inch stubble remained when the storm was over. The grain laid on the ground. There would be no harvest because there was no standing crop. There would be no money to put in the bank. The cash cropping wheat growing operation was completely wiped out!

Grandmother had become pregnant again and was having a very difficult time of it. She needed hospitalization and so she was loaded aboard the train for Dickenson, North Dakota, once again. Pop followed overland with the well drilling rig. On October 2, 1914, grandmother gave birth to their second child, also a son, my father, Kenneth R. Freitag.

Pop again drilled wells successfully in and around the Dickenson area. He was able to cover the hospital charges. Even if he had continued to drill, he still would have been unable to make up the financial loss they faced back on the homestead. Considering their tenuous financial situation, the successful well drilling in Dickenson only served to delay the inevitable disaster they would face back in Vananda.

Once back in on their homestead, the harsh realities of life on the Montana prairie set it. Back-to-back crop failures, the lack of success in the well drilling business in Montana and its related expenses proved to be too much. They stayed into the early winter months until all of the money they had left finally ran out completely. The Freitag's were flat busted – BROKE!

Completely downtrodden, anxious and desperate, Pop wired back to relatives in Green County, Wisconsin, begging for help to get out of this debacle. A relative, who remains unknown, wired him the money to move back to Wisconsin. The trip back east to Wisconsin would be vastly different from the trip west a few years earlier. Neither high spirits, nor hopes, nor wishes, nor dreams were present on this trip. At best, this was a trip of escape from a desperate situation- a journey of retreat from the shame of risking it all and losing. This trip back to Wisconsin put an end to the harsh realities of a failed endeavor.

The unnamed relative sent just enough cash to bring a boxcar load back to Wisconsin – but nothing more. Pop loaded the remaining cattle and horses, some furniture and machinery, two infant sons, one wife and himself aboard the boxcar in the bitter cold of the western prairie for the humbling trip back east. Because of his devastating financial defeat and his inability to secure more funding, he knew that whatever would not fit in that single boxcar would have to be abandoned at the homestead. Among those items left behind was his pride and joy, his business passion, the well drilling machine. It would remain parked next to the sod house where he had drilled his first of many unsuccessful wells in Montana. Never again would my grandfather drill a well.

Never again would he touch the controls of this machine he so loved to operate.

Unwilling to face his successful relatives in Green County, he moved his family and few remaining possessions to the Oshkosh area in east-central Wisconsin. Here he would attempt a new beginning and rebuilding his finances. He rented a farm, basically as a sharecropper, and started all over again.

My grandfather would go on to be involved many different businesses. But never again would he summon up the courage – the guts – to take big risks as a businessman. His entrepreneurial spirit, that certain courage required of risk-takers, was shattered forever. Besides my grandfather abandoning his well drilling machine, he completely abandoned his passion for risk-taking, entrepreneurship and free, private enterprise as well. After his Vananda debacle, my grandfather was not only *broke – he was a broken man*. His venturing fire had been burned out trying to make his Montana dream work. He would never "get back in the game".

When my sister and I were just kids, dad took our family out west to Montana. At Forsyth, we drove 20 miles northwest on U.S. Highway 12 and turned right into the remnants of Vananda located just off the highway. At that time, an elderly couple were the only residents of Vananda. They were living (I imagine squatting) in the old bank building in what remained of the town. Sighting the old guy outside the bank building, my dad went over to him and struck up a conversation. The old-timer actually had known my grandparents and really knew the area very well. He led us out over the prairie and showed us the location of the Freitag homestead. My dad recognized the property immediately as he had come to Vananda in search of his roots in his later teenage years. At the time of my dad's initial visit, when he found the property, some of the larger metal castings of grandfather's beloved well drilling rig were still there next to the caved in sod house.

Today, the remains of Vananda, Montana, can still be viewed from U.S. Highway 12. Some Montana road maps still denote the little town, many do not. All that remains on the townsite is a decrepit old two-story brick school building, some remaining building foundations and some scattered debris. The old brick Vananda Bank building has been moved twenty miles down the road and now sits in downtown Forsyth. There is a historic plaque on that relocated bank building telling the history of a city that once was.

I have visited Vananda a few times and find its history to be fascinating given my tie to the area through my grandparents failed attempt at homesteading.

For some time now, all that remains of Vananda, Montana, is an authentic western ghost town. The town where my grandfather abandoned his dream – where he went BROKE - would become abandoned as well.

The two-story brick school building and the remnants of Vananda, Montana, viewed looking east from U.S Highway 12.

The Vananda State Bank Building which has been relocated to downtown Forsyth, Montana.

BROTHERS IN BUSINESS

In 1932, Grandmother passed away. Pop married for a second time in 1936 to his first wife's second cousin in east-central Wisconsin. His second wife wanted to get out of her career as a public health nurse. She wanted to be in the nursery business for some reason and steered the family in a new direction. It happened that her father had been in the nursery business in west-central Wisconsin at Eau Claire some years before.

In the early 1920s, three individuals had started a small nursery business in Western Wisconsin. Pop's new father-in-law was one of the original signatories to the Articles of Incorporation for the Menomonie-Eau Claire Nurseries, Inc., dated December 2, 1927. The firm had been operated as a three-way partnership for a few years prior to the formation of this new corporate business structure.

Twenty-two months after incorporating, a very famous event occurred which had an impact not only on this newly formed fledgling corporation, but on the world of business globally. The New York Stock Exchange crashed on October 29, 1929. Four months after the crash, Eau Claire County Courthouse records note a name change from Menomonie-Eau Claire Nurseries, Inc. to Eau Claire Nurseries, Inc. on January 15, 1930. Neither the name-change nor any other actions taken by the Board of Directors could do anything to remedy the collapse of the world-wide economy. The corporation went BROKE!

The bank holding the mortgage notes took over the assets of the corporation including the farm on which the nursery stock was being grown. This farm had previously been owned by Pop's father-in-law and had been used as collateral for him to obtain his corporate stock.

Pop's new wife, who had been a spinster into her mid-forties, took out loans against her life insurance policies to buy the farm back from the bank. The purchase offer was accepted and the deal signed. The Freitag's, brother Ed, Kenny and their younger sister Lois along with Pop moved from the eastern side of the state to the western side of Wisconsin to begin a new venture in the nursey business. Pop's wife stayed behind as she had to fulfil her contractual obligation as a public health nurse to her employer, Calumet County.

In starting this new enterprise, they discovered that, although the Eau Claire Nursery, Inc. was bankrupt, the paperwork forming the Articles of Incorporation were yet intact and registered. The corporation was in a state of dormancy. So, when the new owners started anew, they kept the latest corporate name for the business and started over. Eau Claire Nursery, Inc. was back in business but under new ownership.

The farm to which the family moved was a "has been" nursery in every respect. All of the nursery stock, which had been abandoned as far as plant maintenance was concerned due to the bankruptcy of the business several years before, was basically an entangled jungle. There had been no root pruning, no shaping and no trimming for the past several years since the property was totally neglected when owned by the bank. What should have been individual specimen plants was just a mass of overgrown thicket.

The decision was made to uproot everything and start over with fresh seedlings and saplings. The two Freitag brothers worked with a team of horses pulling all of this tangled mess out of the ground to be burned. This would make room for new stock which arrived and was planted. Problem! Now what to do? You cannot make a living waiting and watching trees and shrubs grow to a marketable size – this process takes some time.

That winter, Pop and his two sons, Ed and Kenny, worked in the forests of western Wisconsin as lumberjacks. Their younger sister, Lois, though only a teenager, was made to do housekeeping, cooking and cleaning at the farm.

Spring came and the trees and shrubs in the nursery were not yet marketable, naturally. Now what to do? The decision was made to buy out a cattle hauler who had a regular route in the area. The brothers drove the cattle trucks hauling livestock to the cattle yards in South St. Paul, Minnesota, and hauling groceries back to Eau Claire. They were in business, more or less, but only getting by – not really getting ahead.

A local home builder stopped by the nursery one day looking for someone with a team of horses and a "slip-scraper" to dig a basement for a new home. The brothers jumped at the opportunity. Neither brother had any idea of how to go about the business. But they were young, tough, determined to succeed and had no shortage of ambition or willingness to learn.

This was a totally new type of business. They did know how to work with a team of horses and hoped that knowledge would carry the day. They succeeded in digging and then backfilling that first basement which launched them into a new enterprise. Now the family was in the nursery business, the cattle trucking business and the excavating business.

Ed and Kenny must have done a good job on that first basement because other area home building contractors began to call them about excavating and backfilling basements. They soon found out that no matter how young you are, how ambitious you might be, even how much you enjoy backbreaking labor, digging and backfilling basements with a team of horses and a "slip-scraper" not only gets old but makes an old man out of you in a hurry. Taking turns alternating working with the team or cleaning out the corners of the excavation with a hand shovel, the two brothers knew there had to be a better, easier, more efficient way to work less hard physically, get more done in less time and make this new enterprise more profitable.

A traveling machinery salesman, a Mr. "Zerk" Taylor from Hunter Machinery Company of Milwaukee, Wisconsin, was looking for business in west-central Wisconsin. He found the boys one day and noted that he couldn't tell if the horses or the boys were sweating the most.

He proceeded the show the Freitag brothers some sales literature on a Northwest Model 18 Power Shovel – a crawler mounted excavating machine made in Green Bay, Wisconsin, by the Northwest Engineering Company. Whether it was the heat, the sweat, the dust, the misery of it all or just plain good old-fashioned salesmanship, Ed and Kenny decided to buy the machine. They had no money to speak of for the down payment. Taylor, the salesman, himself made the down-payment on the machine for the boys when the deal was signed. He must have really trusted the boys or felt sorry for them. At the time, when the order for the power shovel was placed, there was a waiting period of 18 months before the machine would be delivered. During the waiting period, Ed and Kenny kept on digging and backfilling basements the hard way with the horses and "slip-scraper".

When not excavating or cattle hauling, the brothers bid on a variety of projects in either nursery work, landscaping, trucking or excavating. They landed a project for landscaping work on a scale they had never done up to that time. Their bid was accepted by the U.S. Army Corps of Engineers to do all the sodding, seeding and planting of trees and shrubbery at three of the new locks and dams being constructed on the upper Mississippi River. These three projects were really their first highly profitable work. For the first time since starting in business in western Wisconsin, they had a little cash with which to operate.

However, when the new Northwest Model 18 Power Shovel was finally delivered, the company was again basically without sufficient cash due to ever increasing payrolls which were tied directly to the expansion of the enterprise. Although the down-payment had been made, it was necessary to pay Hunter Machinery Company in full for the machine. Precariously thin finances would remain a recurring theme throughout the existence of the business.

These youngsters needed credit at a bank. But they were unfamiliar with banking and knew nothing about financing or how to get it or even how to establish credit. The brothers could prove that they had long lists of customers who wanted work done. They could prove that the work would be profitable even doing the work the old way with horses. The machinery company, however, wanted cash, not lists or excuses. Mr. Taylor, from Hunter Machinery Company introduced Ed and Kenny to a local banker whom he knew. Through this introduction, the brothers got the machine financed. Needing all their other assets for the day-to-day operations of the company, they traded in the team of horses. (I've always pictured a machinery sales lot with two old sway-backed nags tied to a hitching post amid all sorts of machinery and power equipment.)

With the new power shovel, instead of taking three days to dig a basement, they were now able to dig two basements in three days. Productivity on this scale was unheard of at the time in their area of operation. Word of this efficiency spread rapidly within the building contractor's circles. The jobs poured in. Contractors from up to fifty miles away were calling asking to be placed on the list without even asking for price quotations. Now, additional excavating equipment was needed to keep up with the ever-increasing demand for their service. More trucks were added to the fleet and different types of equipment was needed. A Caterpillar crawler loader and bulldozer, draglines and heavy-haul tractor-trailer rigs were needed to move an ever-expanding fleet of excavating equipment. All of these new additions to the fleet could not be purchased from cash reserves. There were no cash reserves.

Soon the Freitag brothers were on a first name basis with the bankers. Debt financing was the only way to expand a cash starved business and that is how they made their business grow to serve the needs of their ever- expanding clientele. More business required more vehicles and equipment which could only be accomplished with more debt. Strong financial statements based on cash flow and the continued expansion and growth kept the bank willing to go along with the increased debt load.

Commercial building contractors, not just home builders, were soon utilizing the services of the growing business. This new commercial work and the resulting increase in the size of the projects required the firm to purchase additional equipment to handle the increasing size and complexity of the projects. Heavy earth moving equipment was added to the fleet as site grading projects became another line of work. Crane service, for-hire heavy hauling, aggregate production and other lines of work tied to the commercial building industry were added as the need arose. The expanded equipment fleet required the expansion of the repair and maintenance facilities. Several repair shop buildings and storage buildings were constructed on the farm/nursery property to accommodate this growth.

At the time, it appeared that the business was really starting to come together for the Freitag brothers and Eau Claire Nursery, Inc., However, the world started to come apart. It was the dawn of World War II.

Thirty-eight trucks, five cranes, eight crawler tractors, three road graders, six earthmovers, three heavy-haul tractor-trailer rigs, two power shovels, five farm tractors, three front end loaders - all purchased with debt financing. Each and every piece of equipment and every vehicle needed fuel to operate and now fuel became a rationed commodity. Additionally, the building materials used by the building contractors were rationed due to the war effort.

It became obvious that in order to survive under these new conditions, it was necessary to remake the business into something that was needed by the government. The business needed government contracts. Private industry was all but shut down. So, the question became one of how do we get involved in the war effort?

Trucks were contracted to haul logs to a plywood manufacturing factory in northern Minnesota. Trucks were contracted to haul special filter sand to Chicago. Cranes and other heavy equipment were kept busy working to remodel and retool area factories for war materials production. One way or another, the Freitag brothers kept the operation afloat by keeping the cash flow flowing. This was no simple task in a business which operated on so many rationed commodities. Fuel and tires were always in short supply. Worse yet was the problem of finding the repair parts necessary to keep the truck fleet on the road. Fortunately for the firm, Ed liked Ford trucks and the fleet was nearly standardized with Ford Motor Company vehicles. The significance of this standardization is that the interchangeable parts allowed the firm to keep more vehicles running even if one or two were "cannibalized" to keep the other trucks operational. During that time, it was not possible to go to a Ford Motor Company dealership and purchase whatever you needed in the way of repair parts. There were few if any repair parts available. The brothers came to be on a first name basis with all the Ford dealers within a one-hundred-mile radius of Eau Claire. For example, one dealership may have a set of piston rings, another eight connecting rods, yet another a cylinder head, or a few pistons. Many miles were traveled to accomplish what had, prior to the war, taken only one trip to the local dealer.

Early in 1942, when the outcome of World War II hung in the balance, Kenny was drafted into the U.S. Army. Despite the fact that his left hand was only a thumb and a little finger due to an industrial accident in his youth, he was never-the-less called to duty. He was never stationed further from home than Fort Sheridan, Illinois, (just north of Chicago) due to his handicap. But he and others with a less than perfect bodies, served until the outcome of the war was obvious enough that he and the others could be sent home. He was always angry that he never got sent overseas saying, "I could shoot just as well as any of those guys with two good hands."

Ed was exempted from military service so that he could continue to run the business which had government contracts to fulfil. Ed took on a wide range of projects including several airport runway grading jobs, one way off in the Kansas City area. Ed was keeping the business operational though and that was the point.

Discharged prior to the war being over, Kenny took employment with other area firms. Had he gone back to the family business, Ed's military exemption would have become void and Ed would certainly have been drafted. Because Kenny was "out of the picture" during his time in uniform and Ed had all the contacts and knew all the details of the day-to-day operations, it only made sense to keep Ed in control of the business.

With the end of the war, came new hopes for bigger and better things to come for the firm which was held together in spite of the hardships during the war. Kenny was now back with the firm and work was coming in from the private sector like never before. The post-was housing boom, revamping of factories back to non-military, pre-war production, along with a number of public works projects made the firm grow and expand once again. The days of rationing were a thing of the past and trucks and machinery, building supplies – everything – was becoming available after the four-year long war-mandated hiatus. Better yet, war surplus trucks and machinery were available at public auctions around the country. This made equipment acquisition very simple. After the years of waiting for or doing without needed equipment, this new ease of expansion was like a dream come true.

But hidden in this dream was a problem – a big problem – one that the brothers never had faced until now.

With the end of the second world war, vast numbers of ex-G.I.'s returned home looking for employment or business opportunities. This situation gave rise to a heretofore unheard-of phenomenon for the Freitag brothers – a lot of competition!

The new post-war housing and commercial building boom caused the demand for the services provided by Eau Claire Nursery, Inc. and their few other pre-war competitors to swell beyond these firm's capacity to perform the work. To fill this void, returning ex-G.I.'s rushed into the market. Based on their war-time experience, these ex-G.I.'s had been trained by the military to operate excavation and grading equipment. This was no huge leap of faith for them to transition into the private sector to do this same sort of work on their own. Just like the Freitag brothers, if able to secure financing, they too could attend these government sponsored public auctions and purchase machinery and trucks. All you had to do was be the high bidder and write a good check no matter what your name was.

This new market situation had never before been experienced. The earth moving market became flooded with excavators. Pricing to do the work plummeted. The basement excavation and backfilling business, once 90% controlled in the area by the Freitag brothers, became a market in which they could no longer afford to operate given the savage competition from these new, hungry competitors. While the Freitag's were actually businessmen based on their ten plus years of experience, they were more than aware of maintenance, upkeep and replacement costs of machinery and vehicles for the excavating business given their history prior to the war. These new guys may well have been good equipment operators, but they had no idea of any of the real costs associated with the business they were now involved in. To put it bluntly, these new competitors were wage earners who were buying themselves a job. Therefore, so many were working for little or nothing other than wages and fuel for their machines. That's tough competition. Attrition finally thinned the ranks of these startup enterprises as one after another went broke. When their money was gone and their machinery worn out, they had nothing left with which to repair or replace their machines. They were finished.

While all of this competitive savagery was going on, the Freitag's decided they had to change their business structure in order to survive. They looked over their entire business operation and determined which facets of the business to pursue and which to jettison.

First to go was the cattle hauling business along with the cattle hauling trucking authority granted by the State of Wisconsin. The smaller excavation equipment was either sold off or traded in to purchase larger machinery with which to do larger grading projects. Contracts were sought which placed the firm in markets in which most all of these new "upstarts" could not compete. Basically, the idea was either to work in areas of the market where competition was not likely or to do the type of work where there actually was little or no competition at all. The plan worked – at least for a while.

During the Freitag's operation of the Eau Claire Nursery, Inc. it became basically a partnership operation run by the two brothers. Although it was Pop's second wife who had secured the financing to purchase the property on which the business was located, neither Pop nor his wife were interested in the management nor the operations of the business. However, I'm told, they were excellent at criticism of the operations and any and all decisions being made by the brothers.

With neither of the senior Freitag's wanting actual involvement in the day-to-day operations of the firm, why had Pop's wife financed the purchase of the property which had been used as collateral for so many of the business asset purchases over time? Apparently, she made her decision to buy the property back from the bank only because her father *had owned it in the past*. Perhaps she simply wanted a familiar place to move to when they left eastern Wisconsin.

In late 1949, the board of directors of Eau Claire Nursery, Inc., (Ed, Kenny and their wives) decided to pay off the two people who had made the firm possible financially – Pop and his wife. To remove these two from even their limited involvement in the business and not to have to listen to any more of the criticism whatsoever, a cash settlement of $40,000.00 was paid. Pop and his wife moved out of the area, back to Monticello, Wisconsin. Sadly, the brothers simply ignored their little sister's involvement and the effort she had contributed to the enterprise. She had married a dairy farmer and moved onto his farm. There is no excuse for the brothers to completely disregard her efforts and to basically steal from her any portion of the enterprise to which she may have been entitled because of her contributions to the business. Aunt Lois was paid nothing and that is shameful.

Buying out Pop and his wife resulted in two very important developments for the firm and the brothers/partners. The buyout gave the two brothers complete control of the business (their wives were not involved at all) and the buyout also resulted in the depletion of virtually all of the firm's working capital. Since this dangerous fiscal position close to insolvency was pretty much the norm anyway, the brothers knew this situation could be overcome as it always had in the past.

Except, as happens so often in partnerships, the partners began to *hate*, to *loathe* one another!

PARTNERSHIP NO MORE!

It was bound to happen. But why and why then? What caused the partnership to come apart at a time when it would seem as though everything in the business was finally fitting together rather nicely? Except, of course, for the fiscal situation. Was there a primary cause for the split or were there a number of factors that ultimately caused the brothers to agree to disagree?

Again, basically I have three sources available to use as references with which to formulate answers these questions.

By all accounts, there was no shortage of work for the company. Ed had many contacts in the building trades circles throughout west-central Wisconsin and used these contacts to solicit projects in the area. Public works projects were generated through the competitive bidding process. Road construction projects as well city street grading jobs were the type of work sought by the firm. There were still a few loyal home building contractors from the earlier days who would employ the firm for basement excavation and backfilling. Area township boards would hire Eau Claire Nursery, Inc. to grade and surface township roadbeds. Aggregate production, primarily road gravel processing, was keeping the truck fleet busy. Landscaping and lawn work along with nursery product sales were booming. All of this was directly tied to the explosive growth in the post-war housing boom.

So, with all facets of the business seemingly going in the right direction, in the midst of all of this business activity, what went wrong?

Many factors entered into a complex formation of events which spelled the end of the brother's partnership. At the root of all the problems lied the old company nemesis from day one – money. More explicitly, the lack of it. Then too, the inability to of the brothers to rationally communicate with one another on how best to utilize the limited funds available seems to have been the fuse which ignited the final blowout.

Certainly, other factors played a role in the breakup as well. But primarily two strong willed, stubborn, bull-headed individuals who lacked the ability to compromise their own personal viewpoint in the interest of the larger corporate picture did not help the situation. The simple basic fact that brothers were openly warring with each other around business headquarters caused a breakdown in the level of commitment to the firm for both employees and customers. Employees began to take sides as though preparing to do battle with the opposition. The age-old idea of "equal partnership", as in this case, all too often does not last because of petty jealousies and resentments which develop between the partners. One partner, or both, feel they are "carrying the load" while the other is contributing little or nothing to the enterprise. This individual jealousy often times leads to a deeper sense of suspicion, further resentment and finally hatred. Hatred was the determining factor which brought an end to the firm.

Ed and Kenny fought about which direction the firm should move within the markets they served. Each brother felt his portion of the firm's business was more worthwhile, more profitable, more important than his brother's. Business decisions were made by one brother without the benefit of conversation with his equal partner. This was business gone mad! Under these conditions, it was inevitable that a total financial collapse was just around the corner. Operating or, in this case, failing to operate a business under these conditions is catastrophic.

It did not take too much of this warring and it did not take too much time before the firm's cash position dropped to the point where it became impossible to pay the bank and other creditors. Always under-capitalized from the beginning, this drop in operating funds forced the hard facts to come to the forefront. The firm had assets but insufficient working capital to make payroll, to pay creditors and to continue operations. The brother's rivalry escalated. The Eau Claire Nursery, Inc. was BROKE!

Realizing it would be pointless to attempt to continue to operate the business under the existing conditions, and believing that a liquidation of the corporate assets would pay off all of the creditors, the warring brothers finally did agree on one thing – holding a public auction. All of the trucks, all of the machinery, even all the miscellaneous small tools and specialty equipment was cleaned, painted and lined up for the sale. A multitude of the company's creditors garnisheed the sale to be assured of payment of old accounts.

The auction sale was held. After the sale, all of the various creditors were paid in full. The Freitag brothers split the $34,000.00 left over after cleaning up all of the outstanding debts.

On January 14, 1953, after nearly 20 years in business, the Freitag brothers still had the old nursery property and $17,000.00 each – not much to show for 20 years of very hard work. Their inability to get along with one another caused their business demise. The Articles of Incorporation of The Eau Claire Nursery, Inc. remained on the courthouse records though it was, once again and at best, a dormant corporation. Each brother decided to go his own way. Kenny bought Ed's half interest in the old nursery property and would go on to start over in the business that he knew. Ed would go on to become involved in a large aggregate production enterprise in Michigan's upper peninsula. They rarely spoke of or to one another again except to snarl contempt for each other until they died. Each brother knew in his own mind that it was his brother's fault which caused the end of the Eau Claire Nursery, Inc.

Although they had gone BROKE, they would both start in business anew. Neither brother's risk taking, entrepreneurial spirit was *broken*.

PART II – FAMILY BUSINESS

SOLE PROPRIETORSHIP

No older brother to listen to. No corporate partnership. No work and, of course, no working capital. It was under these conditions that Kenny would start over again in business, but this time, on his own.

Because Kenny bought out Ed's share of the old nursery property, his working capital was virtually depleted. He wanted to continue to be in the same type of business he had been in with his brother. However, this is difficult without trucks, machinery and equipment. He had none. To re-enter the market, he would need to purchase the equipment necessary to do the type of work he knew and understood best.

To acquire equipment, it was back to the old repeating theme – pledge the farm as collateral and borrow the money from the bank. He had not been debt-free from his last business venture long enough to really fully appreciate the comfort of this new debt-free lifestyle. Once again, he plunged back into the financial situation he had been in not so long ago.

During the last year or so of the Eau Claire Nursery, Inc., while Ed had been busy with the commercial building contractors and public works contracting, Kenny became involved in a new and unique, highly technical grading construction type of work. The rejuvenated, highly mobilized post-war American public became addicted to anything having to do with the automobile. The newfound auto addiction gave rise to any number of new industries dependent upon autos, one of which was the completely new concept of drive-in movie theaters.

Prior to the breakup of the partnership, Kenny had graded several of these newly popularized types of theaters. He had built a reputation of doing this new line of work efficiently both cost-wise and time-wise. This reputation would follow him into his new enterprise.

The outdoor theater grading business was perfect for Kenny. This grading did not require the huge debt load that other types of earth moving, such as roadway construction, might necessitate. He only needed a few pieces of machinery to do what needed to be done. Working alongside with a few highly skilled operators, he could do this sort of work with a limited investment, limited payrolls and limited cash outlays. Grading outdoor theaters was Kenny's business plan for how to start over.

The plan worked. Kenny and a business friend of his in the engineering and surveying business had been working together on this outdoor theater grading business from Kenny's initial job. Together they had developed a method for setting the grade stakes (termed "offset staking") which cut the time necessary to do the work. This method eliminated the need to constantly have technical people on site to re-stake the job for finish grading after the rough grading was completed. No outdoor theater goer needed to know this or realize it, however, each one of the sloped parking ramps on these projects was set a different slope angle – the steepest slope being the front row. Each row back dropped in slope angle to facilitate viewing the screen. Given this fact, this was indeed highly technical, very intricate grading. Competitors would need to re-stake each individual ramp but Kenny and his surveyor friend had figured out a better, quicker, more efficient method and this method and the competitive edge it made possible would yield positive results.

Outdoor theaters construction was a fad. When the fad was in full swing, solicitations for construction services came Kenny's way. He would travel the entire state of Wisconsin grading outdoor theater projects – from the southern to the northern boarders, from the east to the west. With this unique staking method and the resulting efficiencies this generated, not to mention his experience in this intricate kind of grading, he was able to win bids beating local area grading contractors wherever he went in the state. Despite the fact of being low bidder on these projects, he was really making money. He knew his costs and he knew his margins. The formula was working.

That first year on his own, he operated under the old firm name. Even though the old corporation was dormant, his thinking was that there would be name recognition in the industry. In 1955, the old dormant corporation was given life again as well as a name change to Kenneth R. Freitag, Inc. This new corporate name and he himself personally were now becoming synonymous with outdoor theater grading. He felt he should capitalize on this personal tie-in with the business. It worked.

He had planned on grading outdoor theaters for the balance of his business career but this was not to be. As with all fads, the outdoor theater grading business came to an abrupt end as the market for this work became saturated around the state.

Though he possessed a great deal of knowledge about grading and grading equipment and had a highly skilled crew, with the end of the outdoor theater grading fad he had come to rely on – now what?

His answer this time was township road grading and surfacing. He knew he was not equipped to compete for the large state highway projects. He became very aggressive in this township (rural) road grading business. During the winter months when earth moving construction is all but impossible in the frozen earth of Wisconsin winters, he traveled a 50-mile radius of Eau Claire selling his services to all the town chairmen in the area. He was thorough enough in his sales efforts to be on a first name basis with the majority of the town chairmen in his targeted market area. Once again, this dedication to his sales efforts paid off well. The work came his way.

During those times, these sales effort were necessary because township work was not based on competitive bidding. This work was more or less granted by the town board and the town chairman. Contacts, *not contracts*, were the main method of obtaining these jobs. Good references and a recommendation from one town chairman to another were the path to success. Kenny got plenty of good references which assured a continuing workload. Not only did the workload continue, it increased handsomely. More work got more references which got more work.

This increased workload made it necessary, once again, to purchase additional equipment. Bankers could now look at a proven track record of debt reduction along with sound financial statements. They were now willing to go along with financing additional equipment purchases. Kenny was more cautious than he had been in the past with debt financing. He would only add equipment to the fleet when he felt totally comfortable with any debt this time around. Some years he would only add a piece or two or he would trade a vehicle for a newer model to improve the reliability of the equipment lineup. The township work was sustaining this company growth.

One evening during this time when Kenny was in the office, an area bridge building contractor stopped in looking for a grading contractor to work with him on state projects. Bob Hindman, a third-generation bridge building contractor from Glenwood City, Wisconsin, told Kenny he had checked around and had heard only good comments about Kenny, his business and the way he and his crews did their work. He told Kenny he was interested in building a solid working relationship with a reputable and reliable grading contractor and through this "quasi-partnership", both firms could benefit nicely.

Kenny did not – *did not* – jump at this opportunity. He was very apprehensive. This bridge builder would need to convincingly answer an array of questions before this conversation would continue in the direction it had taken so far. Why would an experienced bridge building contractor like Hindman want to deal with a small-time, non-entity guy like Kenny in the state road grading business? How could a small firm which did not own the large equipment for large scale highway projects compete in the fiercely competitive state road building game?

Back in the days of the Eau Claire Nursery, Inc., brother Ed had always handled the bidding on state projects. Kenny had no idea of how to go about this style of bidding. How was he going to be able to bid these projects and do the work without getting hurt financially? There were plenty of highway contractors going broke all the time. There was so much to know to do this type of work and he had no teacher. Who would mentor Kenny on the finer points of doing state highway work?

Bob Hindman's answer came straight to the point. Hindman had, in the past, always had to rely on the large earth moving contractors to do the earthmoving and grading for the bridge approaches on his projects. Since these jobs were basically considered to be of little or no consequence by the large earth moving contractors, Hindman was forced to wait for them to show up on his projects all too many times. Waiting for these larger contractors to show up on the job when they more or less felt like showing up, had caused delays on his projects which did not set well with him. Since he concentrated on the smaller scale jobs which he claimed were more profitable, he was only interested in building bridges, not on earth moving or the ownership of large equipment. On these smaller jobs, the sort Hindman sought, Kenny's equipment would be of adequate size to do everything required on these projects. The larger equipment owned by the big contractors often were oversized to do what was required on jobs which Hindman built. The old bridge builder would coach, teach, instruct and generally mentor Kenny and help him learn the state road building business. Bob would help his mentee formulate the bid pricing on the earthmoving portion of the work. On the job he would teach his mentee how to deal with the state highway engineers and inspectors. With these questions answered in a straight forward manner, Kenny agreed to give this new line of work a try.

Together they toured several upcoming job sites. At each site, they discussed how best to tackle the job and how to lay out an orderly sequence of operations. How could one firm help the other when both were on the job at the same time? What arrangements on the job would keep each firm's equipment out of the others way? Basically, these discussions were about efficiency, reducing costs and cutting time. They made extensive notes about each job. They would need these notes.

A strong bond of mutual trust and respect developed between the two men. This bond, this trust grew as they traveled to the state highway bid letting in Madison, Wisconsin, where the contract awards were made.

Once in Madison, it quickly became obvious to Kenny that the old bridge building contractor not only knew a lot of people in the industry, but really knew the "ins and outs" of the state road contracting game. Bob spent a lot of time introducing Kenny around in the circles of contractors involved in the various highway contracting practices.

Bob and Kenny worked together in the hotel room figuring and refiguring their bids on the projects they were bidding together. They had to get as competitive as possible while remaining profitable. Again, and again, they would pour over the notes they had taken at the various project sites and then re-adjust the figures. Hindman then tutored Kenny on the finer points of state contracting, teaching him how to fill out the bid tabs in the most advantageous manner. Exhausted, at around 3:00 p.m., both men retired for the night. At the bid letting the following morning, Hindman and his mentee succeeded winning several projects as the low bidders.

More important than winning these contracts was the fact that Kenny had his eyes opened to a vast array of business opportunities available in the public works sector of the economy. This was a new arena of possibilities for him since his brother Ed had always handled this type of work during the partnership era of the past.

As a 'first-timer" and a new player in the public road contracting business, he had a lot to learn. Project acceptance was no longer as simple as a nod or a handshake from a town chairman. State highway engineers with detailed plans and specification books clearly spelled out what was acceptable, or what "met specs", and what did not. Project engineers would require samples of materials to be used, check soils for compaction density and verify grade elevations. They would maintain a constant oversite of the project from beginning to end and would check in from time to time. This constantly being watched was totally new for Kenny and it was unnerving for him, but not so for the old bridge builder. This nervousness on the part of his new earth mover mentee must have been very noticeable to Bob.

As the first project came near to completion, Bob took his novice for a drive to review the project. Having been through these final inspections many times before himself, Bob was confident of the completeness of the project and sure that all of the work would, as was slang for this project close-out, "meet specs". He told Kenny that these state engineers were likely to be extra critical of his work given that he was a rookie and that this was his first outing on projects of this nature.

Kenny was "rattled" already and then to hear this from Bob only made things worse. While Kenny was more than certain of the skill of his operators and the quality of the workmanship they had done on the job, never the less, he was worried about the inspection.

The old bridge builder told Kenny that these guys were going to sight down all of the shoulder lines, check all the grades, make sure that all of the edges were just so, check all slope angles, measure shoulder widths. The inspectors would try to find any little thing which was not absolutely perfect. Now Kenny was really shaken. All of this was going to happen, however…

The old contractor told Kenny not to be so worried about the inspection. He knew they were going to pass the inspection without one glitch. But how could this to be?

Bob told Kenny he was going to show him an old trick his dad had taught him. Used time and again, it was a sure way to pass inspections every time with limited grief from the engineers. He told Kenny that his dad had called this trick the "old decoy tactic".

He told Kenny to leave a pile of debris like stumps, rocks, old tangled fencing wire and fence posts, any kind of ugly junk available on the construction site just at the edge of the backslope at the beginning of the project. Bob wanted to make sure this pile of ugliness was very, very obvious. Bob told Kenny that, after the final inspection was complete, he might have to spend an hour or two with some machinery to clean up this mess, but so what. Kenny didn't understand what was going on, but followed Bob's instructions.

When the inspectors arrived for the final inspection, Bob and Kenny along with the two inspectors loaded themselves in Bob's car to tour the project. As they started down the bridge approach towards the bridge, both engineers suddenly became irate. There sat this ugly pile of debris and junk right off the edge of the backslope. How could these guys have had the nerve to tell the project engineers that this project was completed and ready for final inspection when there was this mess? This ugliness was such an obvious oversight on the part of the contractors. It was a terrible injustice that the engineers had to waste their time to come out to look over a job that was nothing but a mess. They complained on and on about that hideous debris pile for the rest of the project tour. They never wanted to stop to measure anything. It was just the incessant complaining about the pile of trash left at the foot of the backslope.

So, Bob asked the two engineers if the debris was cleaned up, was the rest of the project acceptable? Yes, yes, everything else looked just fine except for that ugly, hideous trash heap just off the backslope. If they would just get this mess removed from the project, everything else looked just fine, Bob was told.

Bob told the engineers that they would clean up the mess and invite the engineers back. Sounding apologetic to these two engineers, Bob wondered how he and his rookie grading contractor could have been so careless, so foolish as to leave such an ugly mess on the jobsite? Bob said he'd call them back when the mess was cleaned up.

The debris pile cleanup took just over an hour. Bob called the engineers who said that if the debris pile was indeed gone, as far as they were concerned, the project was complete in every way and final payment would be sent.

What a lesson!

Kenny was fortunate to have had Bob Hindman as his mentor. He was able to learn so much from such an experienced old contractor. These early lessons in dealing with government inspectors and other bureaucrats would serve him well in the years to come.

Since he was learning this new endeavor, the first few jobs of bridge approach construction were marginal, at best, financially. The lack of jobsite know-how caused a number of inefficiencies. He learned quickly and made the necessary corrections in both operational efficiencies and bidding procedures which enabled him to go forward to prosper in this new business.

These earliest jobs were done by Kenny as a subcontractor. The bridge builder was the general (prime) contractor by virtue of his experience and, more importantly, his ability to secure contract bonding which the state mandates on construction projects. To explain this in a simplified fashion, contract bonding certifies to the state that the contractor with the winning bid will fully complete the project per plans and specifications. Should the contractor go broke while attempting to complete the project, the bonding company will pay to have the work completed by another contractor. Of course, the contractor pays a fee to the bonding company for this guarantee.

For these initial projects, Kenny had no ability to secure contractor bonding. Given time and a portfolio of completed projects proving he and his firm could do the work based on that experience, he would be able to bid and bond jobs as a general contractor. But for now, he was just a "sub".

The contacts he had made in Madison, good reports from engineers, more trips to more state bid lettings and a strong desire to expand his business led to contracts with other bridge building contractors. Besides continuing the township work, he now had several crews and machinery spread around the state working for bridge builders other than Bob Hindman exclusively. He was spreading his time too thinly among the various jobsites. He was losing control of his business and he knew it.

He hired a grade foreman/project superintendent. He was able to now delegate some of the responsibilities for jobsite operations and control. This took some of the managerial pressure off of him personally. He was able to regain control of his operations with the help of this foreman.

Expansion came rapidly. Motor scrapers (self-propelled earthmovers) were added to the equipment fleet. Larger trucks, front end loaders, bulldozers and compaction equipment were purchased to keep up the level of service necessary to maintain the explosive growth. Many of these items were purchased from equipment dealers in used condition. They had been traded in on new machines either by other contractors or county highway departments. These machines were subsequently rebuilt by company mechanics at the shop facilities. As usual, these additions to the fleet were purchased utilizing additional debt. The increased debt was no problem for Kenny or his banker so long as the work kept coming. And the work kept coming at a furious pace!

He may well have continued to work as a subcontractor for some time, but he was not satisfied being a "sub" for the rest of his business career. He wanted his own action. He wanted to be the general contractor – the prime contractor. "Sub" – really, the word even sounded demeaning – underling, flunky, beneath, below the other contractor. He was determined to find a way to put an end to this underling category he found himself in presently. He was determined to become a general contractor no matter what it would take to get this done.

Based on several years of doing state highway projects as a "sub", he was able to get an "experience rating" – the first step on the trail to becoming a general contractor. This "experience rating" along with several past years of solid financial records and sound business growth, resulted in his ability to secure contract bonding, though on limited basis at initially. With both the "experience rating" and now the contract bonding, he was in the position he had hoped for and worked so hard to obtain. He was now in a position to do state contracting as a general contractor.

Initially, as a general contractor, he was able to bid on only the smallest projects. He did these tiny jobs for his first few projects. He continued to push the limits of his capacities. He kept increasing the size of the projects he would bid, always looking to expand his capabilities and capacities with regard to both bonding capacity and "experience rating". Within two years of beginning this quest to become a general contractor, Kenny was able to tackle the size project he had always been dreaming of.

KENNY'S DREAM JOB

November, 1959. Kenneth R. Freitag, Inc. had just completed the most successful season ever. Never before had there been such a level of sales and profits from a single season's work as was realized that year.

With a construction season like that behind him, his confidence was sky high. His expectations for the upcoming season were so great that he decided to purchase three brand new earthmovers. He would trade in his three older model machines and upgrade his fleet with these newer machines. These machines would add a new level of performance and productivity which could not be realized without "trading up". These new machines would work perfectly and more efficiently for the bridge approach construction business and other smaller grading jobs.

Along with his trade in machines, Kenny would pledge everything he owned as collateral. This included his substantial whole-life insurance policy as well as all of the other machinery, the land and the buildings. His wife (my mother) was not at all comfortable with this decision. But Kenny was not worried at all since business opportunities for the upcoming year looked very promising. Besides, there was always that gambler mutation in his lineage which just seemed to justify his decision. He risked it all and bought the machines.

At the first state bid letting in the spring of 1960, Kenny was particularly nervous about an upcoming project which would be ideal for his firm. The State of Wisconsin had been funding certain county highway regrading-rebuilding projects around the state. One such project was three miles south of Eau Claire. PERFECT!

This project was of the size that would fit the size of his equipment fleet nicely. The project's close proximity to his base of operations made this the project of his dreams. He would push his contract bonding and "experience rating" to the limit if he were successful in his bid for this project. This was the only way to increase the size and scope of future work. Given the closeness of this job, this one "had Kenny's name on it". This was his big chance to expand and he was going to do everything within his power to win the bid on this job.

This time, attending the state bid letting, Kenny was in Madison by himself. He was no longer a "sub", but now a general contractor. He was on his own. was This had been the position that he had been seeking for the past several years. He was determined to succeed. Whatever it took to make his firm grow, he would do it.

Just like all of the previous trips to state bid lettings, he spent all night and half of the early morning hours figuring and re-figuring his bid for the project. This time it was he who was taking price quotations from various subcontractors – not making "sub quotes" and it felt great. He finalized his numbers in the early morning hours and filled out his "practice" bid tab. He felt quite sure that he was low enough to get the work. Yet, there was still a very good profit margin on the project at his final bid price, according to the numbers.

The morning of the actual bid letting couldn't come soon enough. Though the "practice" bid tab was filled out, he could not sleep. Nerves on end, and his mind fried with the figuring and the re-figuring of the project, he could hardly wait for the reading of the bid prices for The State of Wisconsin Highway Department project number SO815 (2), known as the Eau Claire County Highway "F" regrading project.

The questions kept racing through his weary mind. Was his equipment fleet really sizeable enough to handle the six-mile grading project? Or, of the 137,695 cubic yards of unclassified excavation, how much of it would consist of tough rock and how much of it would be merely easy-to-move sand? Did he have enough time and money figured for the clearing of trees and brush? Would the old concrete box culverts and the other metal culvert be demolished in the time and at the cost he had allotted to do this work? And again, had he figured enough for the removal of the little old bridge at station 200+37?

In the back of his mind was the fact that he had collateralized everything he owned to purchase three new earthmovers. He just had to have work - either this job or another one - to keep these new machines operating so that he would be able to make the payments. He had to make the payments – he had to!

Going over the figures one last time, he filled in the unit prices, extended the columns, multiplied, and then added the figures three times. It struck him that this one project was larger than anything ever attempted by the old Eau Claire Nursery, Inc. As a matter of fact, this one project alone involved more money than the total income for an entire year during the best of years of the old firm, even in its finest hour.

Wouldn't it be something if he could win this project? Hardly able to write the final figures on the final bid sheet because of nervousness and the resulting shaking, he got the bid sheet filled out, sealed it in the bid envelope and submitted his bid.

Waiting made the nerves worse. How many projects bids would be read off before they got to project SO815(2)? It was tormenting.

At last! Project SO815(2) bids were read. The low bid was submitter by Kenneth R. Freitag, Inc. of Eau Claire, Wisconsin! HE HAD WON! HE HAD WON! HE HAD WON! Kenny had his dream job! This was his deliverance.

Everything he had worked for in the past all of a sudden made sense. Everything had fit together. He had won his moment of glory. Though he had left quite a margin" on the table" (the difference between the low bid price and that of the next low bidder), he felt confident, fulfilled, euphoric. Now the long drive home would seem an eternity. He could hardly wait to share the good news with his family.

He returned home late that night. No matter. He would awaken the family to share the good - NO! - GREAT NEWS! HE HAD WON! HE HAD WON! Not only had he won, he had won the largest project he had ever attempted in his life. Could everyone grasp the significance of this monumental moment?

Unfortunately, two sleepy children and one sleepy wife were not as enthused as he was at the moment. He would not let their lack of excitement dampen his moment of triumph.

He would go on for days about his victory over much larger firms bidding on the same project. He would tell the story again and again how he had grieved over his bid and then his final "moment of truth" when he reached deep to find the guts to enter that final huge number on the bid sheet. He shared all of this with his family who simply did not understand the significance of what he had accomplished. Though they could little know or understand all of this, they did their best to share his joy and excitement trying to act as if they were as excited about the project as he was.

During the months that followed the bid letting but prior to the construction season, Kenny drove County Highway "F" on a daily basis. He studied the rock face cuts many times along the old roadbed that he, his crew and his machinery were going to regrade. His observations and thinking led him to the conclusion that the south end of the project had some rather tough flintlike sandstone. Maybe he could subcontract this area to one of the area's larger contractors. These larger contractors had heavier bulldozers equipped with rippers to tear through this tougher sandstone. He did not own such equipment. In his present financial condition, with everything already collateralized, he would be unable to borrow another dime with which to purchase a bulldozer with a ripper. Why not "sub-out" this tougher section of the road to one of these "big guys"? He knew what his numbers were. Just maybe, one of these large contractors would be "hungry" and need a job bad enough that they would do the job at a price which would allow him to make a profit from their work.

He found such a firm in his home town. As a matter of fact, it was one of the firms whom he had triumphed over to win the bid.

This firm subcontracted the that section of the project for an unbelievably low price. He was overcome with joy when the larger firm inked the contract for the tough part of the job at such a cheap price, generating him a substantial profit.

The County Highway "F" grading project commenced in early April. Machinery was moved to the jobsite as soon as the "go-ahead" was issued by the Wisconsin Department of Transportation District 6 Office. Barricades were erected, warning flares placed and the clearing portion of the work was started. The field office (a small mobile home) was move to the jobsite. The new earthmovers were put to work and the road grading project of Kenny's dreams started to progress as planned.

A problem soon arose. The new earthmovers were not performing as anticipated. These new machines Kenny had purchased were not the product of the four predominant manufacturers of road building equipment. Rather, they were the product of a smaller, less known manufacturer of heavy equipment. The large four manufacturers used proprietary drive train components. That is to say, that the engines, transmissions and drive axels were designed and manufactured by the company building and assembling the final machines. Not so for this smaller manufacturer from whom Kenny purchased his machines. They utilized vendor supplied components from various sources.

The diesel engines which powered these earthmovers were not really tested in an industrial application of this kind. As a matter of fact, this engine installation was a prototype, an experiment for this model engine. While this engine performed well in over-the-road truck applications, it was incapable of the lower engine speeds and the high initial torque load requirement necessary in earthmoving equipment. These engines were equipped with turbochargers, an exhaust gasses driven form of a supercharger. This was new engine technology at the time. Theoretically, turbochargers increased the horsepower output of the engine if the engine were operating at the governed speed.

The engines were designed to operate at 2100 R.P.M.s. After operating properly for around only four hours or less at the governed engine speed, they would turn out only 1400 R.P.M.s along with plenty of thick, black exhaust smoke. These early turbochargers were thought to be a one-size-fits-all engine add-on. The engines were of a much smaller displacement than other larger engine models offered by this vendor wherein "turbos" had been successful. The "turbo" fans were simply too large to respond quickly when attempting to accelerate the engine under fully loaded machine conditions.

Since the fuel systems were designed and metered at the factory, they had been set up to burn fuel efficiently when turbocharged air was forced into the combustion chamber at a higher density than would be possible without the "turbo". Without the "turbo" coming up to speed quickly enough to burn the fuel efficiently, the unburned fuel would sludge up the fuel injection system resulting in lower performance of the engine. This, in turn, caused the machines to lose power which ultimately resulted in machine performance to be cut to half of what it should have been. The truth is that the performance of these engines was so horrible that it resulted in a lack of efficiency, even created inefficiencies, as the earthmovers underperformed nightmarishly.

The first few times, under warrantee, Kenny had factory trained engine technicians overhaul the fuel systems completely on the machines. But within four hours of overhaul, these engines would simply revert back to their pathetic under performance at 1400 R.P.M.s. They would smoke as though they "were burning soft coal", as one of the operators put it.

Warrantee-wise, the equipment manufacture had the overall warranty on the product. However, the warrantees of the equipment manufacture in conjunction with the engine manufacture became a joke. After sending the engine manufacturers technicians to repair the clogged engines two or three times, finger pointing and accusations of wrongdoing between the engine manufacturer and the machine manufacturer began. The outcome of this denial of responsibility resulted in both firms "washing their hands" of the problem. Nothing more would be done by either manufacturer to help Kenny get his crippled machines fully operational. Since neither manufacturer would accept responsibility for the underperformance, this left a small contractor who had taken a big risk in big trouble.

Kenny considered suing both manufacturers. However, this would not help his immediate problem. As with all State Highway Department contract work, there is a deadline date for project completion. If projects are incomplete on the deadline date, contractors are penalized by being forced to pay "liquidated damages" at a contract fixed price per day basis. Given the project deadline, lawsuits would not solve his dilemma. These cases would not get to court for several years and he only had a few months to get this job completed.

Kenny went to his banker telling him of the problem with the machines and his intention to sue both manufacturers. The banker's response was to inform Kenny how he, the banker, had "gone out on a limb" to help Kenny get the financing to purchase these machines. The banker informed Kenny that he did not know the difference between a turbocharger and a battery charger and that he did not really give a damn so long as Kenny kept on making his monthly payments. If anything should get in the way of Kenny making his monthly payments, then there really would be a problem and that was the only problem that really concerned the banker.

To make those bank payments, Kenneth R. Freitag, Inc. needed to receive "draws" (incremental payments) on the contract from the State Department of Transportation. Obviously, only completed phases of Project SO815(2) would be eligible for such "draws". So, the predicament was as follows; Even if these new earthmovers were only operating at roughly 50% capacity, the desperate need for income from the project along with a job completion deadline forced Kenny to keep going.

Things got worse.

The south end of the project which he had subcontracted to the large firm was going far better than either Kenny or his subcontractor could have imagined. The sandstone on that portion of the job which Kenny thought would be so tough turned out to be of such a soft nature that his subcontractor never had to use the ripper attachment on his bulldozer at all. The stuff simply crumbled. His "sub" was making all sorts of money on his end of the job because of this unexpectedly soft rock.

Another reason for the larger contractor to be more efficient on the job had to do with another factor. The larger contractor had larger machinery and so his efficiency and production were so much greater than Kenny's crew's performance.

The larger contractor was doing well. State mandated wages for operators was the same for those who operated bigger equipment or smaller equipment. For example, if an operator was moving earth with a machine of 30 cubic yard capacity or a machine of 14 cubic yard capacity, the hourly wage paid to both operators was the same. The result of this is that the per-cubic-yard labor cost to move earth was double for the man with the smaller machines as opposed to the man with the larger machines. In truth, Kenny was not properly equipped to handle the size job he had bitten off.

At the same time, Kenny was losing a pile of money on his end of the project. This was not only because of the machinery malfunctions, and the smaller machine size, but production was way off. He had hit some really tough rock. These factors all combined to make this project into "the perfect storm' as production fell way short of expectations.

As it turned out, he had "subbed out" the portion of the project he should have kept and kept the portion he should have "subbed out". He was losing and he was losing bad. He was in big trouble.

I was ten-year-old boy in 1960 when my dad had his dream job going. How well I remember wanting to spend time with my father that summer. Twice I would go to the jobsite with him – only twice. He did not want to be bothered by a boy who loved to see the big machines operate, to smell the diesel exhaust, to hear all of the engines roaring and to see and smell the fresh earth as it was being moved about on the grade. I was only in his way.

My first trip to the jobsite was right after school was out for the summer – early June. Dad was having his problems but not on the scale he would encounter later on in the summer. I can recall my dad discussing problems and brainstorming with his grade foreman to fix the problems. I also recall some rather heated discussions with the project engineer. Other than that, I can only recall what a great time I had watching the big machines roar down the grade, belching great clouds of black exhaust. It was a glorious sight for a roadbuilding contractor's young son who thought that his father's career was about as exciting as any man could possibly wish for. This was an extraordinary day for a boy who longed to spend time with his father. How could things get any better for a kid who loved watching big machines working to build a highway?

The time between the two trips to the jobsite that summer was marked by a severe change in my father's disposition. This change was made evident, obvious even to a ten-year-old, by his sullenness, his somberness and his silence. As the summer progressed and the job situation became worse, my dad's demeanor became downright mean and ugly. A boy who desperately wanted to be like his dad and spend time with him overlooked the ugliness and nastiness as he continued to beg to go along with his dad to the jobsite. That second and last trip that summer to the County Highway "F" job is as fresh in my mind today a if it had taken place yesterday. The memory of that day will live with me to my death.

Dad had come home for lunch just like he did every day that summer. Whether it was my continued begging to go with him or that my mother reminded him that he had a son whom he spent no time with, he grudgingly gave in. I got to go along. I remember how happy I was just to get to go with my dad… well, initially that is.

It was very evident very soon that this was an exceptionally terrible day for dad. It had been raining all day. He drove to the jobsite without uttering a word or even acknowledging my presence on the seven-mile trip from our home. When I attempted to say something, he glared at me. This was definitely nonverbal communication which was clearly understood. It didn't take more than one of these attempts for me to understand that he was totally uninterested in any conversation of any kind with a kid.

Due to the rain, when we arrived at the jobsite, all of the machinery was parked. The crew members were either servicing or making repairs to the machines. Dad calmly asked the foreman where the project engineer was. He was told that the engineer had gone home for the day since the project was shut down because of the weather.

Very quietly in a voice which was so calm that it was unnerving, Dad asked the foreman to have several of the men quit working on the machinery. These men were to go to the old bridge at station 200+37 and dig holes next to the bridge abutments. Today was going to be the day that the bridge would be dynamited and removed.

While the men were preparing the holes for the explosive charges, Dad drove back into town taking me with him. He never uttered a word to me on this trip either. He was acting very spooky. On our way, a cloudburst rainstorm began again. We arrived at the first phone-booth available and he parked the pickup very near the tiny structure at the intersection of U.S.12 and State Street. He got out of the pickup, went to the phonebooth and closed the door behind him. I stayed in his pickup truck with the windows rolled up due to the rain.

I watched my dad as he began to call the telephone company service department. Because of a number of less that pleasant experiences in the past, he hated the telephone company's service department in the worst way to begin with. But on this day, the hatred peaked.

The conversation started off all right, I guess.

Then things took a turn for the worse. Dad was white hot! Instantly his eyes went wild and he began screaming into the phone. How do I know? I heard it through the closed door of the phonebooth, through the closed door of the pickup truck, above the sound of the pounding rain and the highway traffic right next to the phonebooth. I only heard one side of the conversation, of course. And I can only imagine what the poor telephone operator on the other end of the line was saying while trying to reason with this contractor who had obviously gone berserk. Dad began to speak "in tongues". This is a language I too would later become very adept at speaking. I have found that people in all sorts of professions - medicine, law, accounting, teaching, etc., etc., all know and understand this language. This language is not flowery, but certainly colorful. I have come to call this language "CONSTRUCTIONESE".

Just a side note of explanation here; "CONSTRUCTIONESE" is a sub-form of every vernacular language in the world. I've found "CONSTRUCTIONESE" is universally understood because of its simplicity. It is usually delivered to the recipient of a one-sided conversation in a raised tone of voice if not outright hollering. This is purely a results-oriented language with complete and total disregard for the personal feelings, the personal self-mage and personal self-worth of the recipient. It often results in the destruction of all of the afore mentioned. This language deals strictly in communicating desired results and the urgency with which these desired results had better happen. The intricacy of the wording is not so important, rather it is the artistic arrangement of that limited number of four-letter words which give the language its rich flavor. When it's immediate results you are after and interpersonal human relationships be damned, a little "CONSTRUCTIONESE" will get the job done every time. Results come about in a most expedient manner with unclouded clarification of the specific desired actions and the urgency with which these actions had better be acted upon. This demanded immediate action had better take place right now or else...

On that rainy afternoon in the summer of 1960, Dad's voice was not elevated as previously suggested, he was *screaming*. He was using the most violent form of "CONSTRUCTIONESE" I'd ever heard at this poor telephone operator on the other end of the line. I heard the screaming through the glass and the other noise...

"YOU DON'T SEEM TO UNDERSTAND WHAT I'M TELLING YOU, YOU _____ _____ IDIOT! G____ ____, I'M GONNA BLAST THAT _____ _____ BRIDGE RIGHT _____ NOW! I MEAN RIGHT _____ NOW! DO YOU UNDERSTAND RIGHT _____ NOW? I'M NOT TALKING ABOUT TOMORROW OR EVEN LATER THIS _____ AFTERNOON YOU _____ _____ FOOL. I'M GONNA BLOW THAT _____ BRIDGE RIGHT _____ NOW! WHAT EVER HAPPENS TO YOUR ____ _____ _ _____ PHONE LINES AND YOUR _____ _____ PHONEPOLES ARE YOUR _____ PROBLEM! DO YOU HEAR ME, YOU _____ MORON? I DON'T GIVE A GOOD _____ _____ WHAT HAPPENS TO YOUR _____ PHONE EQUIPMENT! IT'S YOUR _____ _____ PROBLEM NOW!"

Some sort of response, and then...

"WHADDYA MEAN YOU'VE GOT 72 _____ HOURS AFTER NOTIFICATION? YOU HAVEN'T GOT 72 _____ SEC-

ONDS! I'M GONNA BLAST THAT _____ BRIDGE RIGHT _____ NOW!"

(*note; you can get creative and fill in the blanks as you see fit. I'm sure you'll come up with something of interest.)

Wild as he was, he slammed the receiver down so hard and with such force that I'm quite certain it was wrecked. He nearly tore the door off the phonebooth as he madly attacked the structure on his way out of it and into the pouring rain. I was scared to death as he nearly ripped the door off the pickup truck and climbed in dripping wet.

Once in the vehicle, he gave me a quick glare and said nothing. I knew I dared not utter a sound. I crouched up in a ball in the corner of the cab. Then his eyes raced wildly about fixing on nothing and yet everything at once. He grabbed the steering wheel, started the pickup and began to back up without checking to see if anyone was behind him. Certainly no one would have dared to be back there. Once backed out of the parking place, something odd, something very, very strange came over him. He hunched over the steering wheel in such a way that his line of vision barely cleared the top of the curvature of the wheel and his eyes were fixed straight ahead. At this point there was no peripheral vision, only that straight-ahead stare fixed ahead but on nothing at all really. It was scary.

To this day I have no idea how we ever got back to the jobsite. But I do remember two distinct things about that trip: 1.) It quit raining and 2.) While Dad was staring as if in some sort of trance, this barely visible sinister little grin developed. It developed into this gruesome, evil Grinch-like smirk which would have inspired Dr. Seuss.

When we arrived back at the bridge, the men had the explosive charge holes ready to be loaded. The smirk clearly there yet, Dad told the men to enlarge the charge holes and to double the number of holes they had prepared. The crew went to work again.

To state that dad overloaded that poor old bridge with explosives would be a huge understatement. To state that he used twice as much explosive as was necessary to do the job would be a second understatement. He kept loading those holes as if he had an unlimited supply of dynamite. Other than muttering a few words to the men, all of the work was done in total silence. He attached the blasting caps, inserted the wire, handed the detonation wire spools to one of the men, and backed his pickup down the road over a quarter of a mile from the bridge. Once there, he raised the hood of the pickup and waited for the man with the wire spools to arrive.

Still, the silence. Still, the fixed gaze. Still the Grinch-like evil smirk. The fixed gaze ended only as he broke that sinister stare to uncover and study the pickup truck's battery terminals for a brief second before touching the detonation wires to the battery terminals. Then…

BOOOM!!!!

Naturally, the larger chunks of concrete came back down to earth first. These larger chunks were followed by smaller and smaller fragments of rubble which had been launched to somewhere just short of the stratosphere. Then, finally, the dust. Oh my, the dust!

When the smoke and dust finally cleared, there was no bridge. There were no phone poles, no phone lines, no power poles, power lines and, for that matter, no forest for some distance around the blast site. Only a massive crater and debris remained where the innocent little old bridge had once stood.

A horde of enraged telephone company personnel arrived on site in less than one half hour. Smirking at all of these angry telephone company service personnel as they marched toward him, Dad said, "See, I knew you guys could be here in less than 72 hours. The next time I call for service, I'll expect promptness just like I got this time because now I know you guys actually can get off your ass and show up to my jobsites quick." (These days, he'd have been shackled and hauled off to jail for this flagrant disregard for utility company assets and public utility authority.)

I was too young to understand back then, but my dad was obviously "fence siting" during that summer of his life. Mentally, he could have gone either way. That is to say, this quasi-stability could have been lost to total madness given the pressure he was under at the time. Fortunately, after the blast, he seemed to regain some kind of mental normality, albeit, a quasi-normality which had escaped him for the months prior to the blast. It is really quite remarkable that my dad's mind did not simply snap.

The stress and pressure continued until the County Highway "F" project was completed. The road building project was completed on time and the project engineer was very satisfied with the workmanship in every way. All was well…

All was well, that is, except for one fact; Kenneth R. Freitag, Inc. was so precariously close to broke that Dad was unable, financially, to do the necessary repairs to his equipment during the winter months following his "dream job". His "dream job" had nearly cost him his company and all the other collateral he had pledged to finance the purchase of the three underperforming machines. Somehow that winter, he kept the bank at bay. But the bank was getting very nervous.

Financially beat up by his "dream job" and now desperate to secure a contract to keep his equipment operating which would generate some cash flow, he contracted to do the site grading work at the new Eau Claire North High School in the spring of 1961. This contract and the promise of a healthy cash flow kept the bank off his back until the money started to move through the company books.

North High School was not a good job either. Problems of all varieties were abundant on this job. There were union problems which plagued the project from start to finish. If the Operating Engineers were not unhappy about something on the project, the Teamsters Union or the Laborers Union were.

The contract called for maintenance of the grassed areas on the job. This meant that the job was acceptable only after the lawn areas were of a suitable thickness of grass to "meet specs". Acres and acres of turf area had to be watered, mowed, clipped and maintained. I know about this. Dad made me, his eleven-year-old son, work along with the rest of his crew doing the watering, and mowing, etc.

When the North High School job was completed, the company did not lose money on the project. But it didn't really make a great deal of money either. Basically, Dad had succeeded only in keeping his crew busy and generating a cash flow. So, the company was still in terrible financial condition and, once again, unable to make the necessary repairs to the equipment. The firm was close to BROKE.

He kept the bank at bay one more winter. By this time, looking over the financial statements, the bankers were beyond nervous. They were fearful of the certain collapse of the business. Somehow, he convinced the bankers to allow him one more season to try to recoup his losses.

During the winter of 1961-62, Dad bid many projects but was unable to secure a single contract. As spring approached with no work, no contracts and very slim prospects of securing a contract, he became frantic. He would hold his company together somehow. The bank would not take him over.

He went to one of the area's larger contractors who had a number of contracts on hand. Dad offered to subcontract a portion of the larger contractor's project on Wisconsin State Highway 29 near Cadott, Wisconsin. Dad's price to do the work had to be lower than the contract bid price by the larger contractor. This allowed the larger contractor to make a guaranteed profit from Dad's work. The deal was negotiated and the contract signed.

The low price to do the work, combined with terrible weather conditions during that summer of 1962, spelled the end of Dad's career as a highway grading contractor. When the "29" job was finished, so was Kenneth R. Freitag, Inc. Dad had gone BROKE! – for a second time!

Toward the end of the job, he informed the bank of his situation, offering to have an auction sale when the job was completed. He asked his bankers and all of his creditors and suppliers to extend him 60 days credit which would allow him to complete the project. He wanted to be a man about it and finish the job himself rather than having the bonding company complete the work at his expense. He did get the job done on his own.

At the completion of the job, all of the machinery was moved back to the base of operations in Eau Claire. Every piece of equipment, every truck, every small tool was cleaned, painted and placed in neat rows in preparation for the auction sale. When the sale was over, Dad paid off the bank and all of his creditors. He was able to keep his land and buildings as well as the life insurance policy he had collateralized. For those employees who could not find employment, he found them jobs - good jobs with area contractor he knew.

Within a nine-year time-frame he had risen from being broke to become quite a contractor only to go BROKE again. Although having gone BROKE for the second time in his career, he was a long way from being a broken man!

Later in life, not too long before he passed away, when I was a businessman myself, he finally spoke about the County Highway "F" project, his "dream job", which he had avoided discussing for so long. He asked me how I would like to go to work every day knowing that, if it was a good day, I would only lose $1000.00 that day. He went on to say that on bad days, losing $1000.00 would seem like a blessing… "That's how things were for me on the County Highway "F" project for better part of that summer", he said.

Oh my GOD!

DIFFERENT DIRECTION

Twice BROKE!

My dad had gone down financially twice at this stage in his career. Even though he had suffered a major loss a for a second time, his entrepreneurial spirit was still intact. He had, however, lost his appetite for the road building contracting business and all the huge risk-taking involved in it. Time to try something new.

The County Highway Commissioner was retiring and the position was going to be open for application. Dad put on a suit and tie for a few days and tried hobnobbing with some of the local county board members whom he knew would have the final say on filling the position. Two days of that politicking and phoniness made him sick to his stomach. He dropped out of that silly pretentious game. He was so sickened by the experience of mingling with these politicians that the thought of working for them was out of the question.

He knew he had to get away from the contracting business because, for now, after getting beat up so badly, he couldn't stand it. He wanted to do something, but basically, he wanted to drop out of sight for a time. He just needed to get away from the business that had nearly driven him insane. He found the perfect pastime to keep him occupied and entrepreneurial. He became a pig farmer.

With the cash remaining after all of the creditors had been paid, he had a pole barn constructed on the old Eau Claire Nursery property.

Farrowing pens were purchased, stalls were built in the barn and the building was made ready for it's new squealing occupants. The majority of the interior work he did himself. This work served several purposes. Certainly, doing the work himself kept the costs to a minimum. Better yet, the physical movement which accompanied such work allowed him to tone his body to a physical condition which he had not experienced in the past twenty years. He was in the feeder pig business for the next year or so. As with any business, he had his good times and his bad times.

He was not allowed to focus on the pig business for too long because the phone started to ring again. A number of old customers and loyal patrons from days gone by started calling to have Dad do their earthmoving. There were small grading jobs on farms. There was residential work for lawn and landscaping installations. Parking lots and driveways to grade and gravel. Town chairmen called wanting road alteration and improvement projects.

Kenneth R. Freitag, Inc. had to re-equip once again. This time there would be no debt financing. If he did not have the funds to purchase a vehicle or machine, he would go without even if it meant turning down job opportunities. Absolutely nothing was purchased new. He purchased cheap, near junk equipment and did a little fixing and repair to make it serviceable. Nothing was fancy, nothing was state-of-the-art. The old trucks he purchased he referred to as his "rainbow fleet". When he bought a truck for instance, if it was red – it stayed red. If it was yellow, it stayed yellow. Whatever color it was at the time of purchase, that was the color it remained. The vehicles and equipment looked terrible but did the job.

Compared to his recent past, he had virtually nothing invested in his equipment fleet. Depreciation schedules reveal that $500.00 was big money for him to pay for any piece of equipment during this time of his rebuilding the company for the third time. He no longer had pride in ownership. He could care less about that. He only had pride in satisfied customers who paid their bills in a timely manner.

Once again, the business started to grow. The feeder pig business was dropped. The hog barn was converted into a repair shop as the equipment fleet kept growing. His reputation was causing him to become a contractor all over again whether he wanted to or not.

A sizable landscape contracting firm from Green Bay, Wisconsin, had submitted the low bid on a huge acreage lawn and landscaping project at the new Sacred Heart Hospital which was being constructed on Eau Claire's south side. The landscape contractor called on my dad because he had been told that Kenny would know where to source many of the materials for the project and that he was the local guy who could get things done.

With limited equipment and a great deal of hard work, this project would afford my dad the finances to rebuild his firm. He contacted every one of his fellow area small contractors and acquaintances whom he felt he could trust, organized those willing to participate in the project, and proceeded to get the work underway. The project progressed rapidly. Given the size of the area to be worked on, much of this work was done using road building sized equipment on this large lawn building project. Lawn grading and landscaping had never been done using that size equipment before in the area. This was a revolutionary idea at the time. But the efficiencies that happened as a result were highly profitable for an entrepreneur who needed to rebuild his firm and, more importantly, his self-confidence. This large-scale lawn job was key to putting him "back on his feet" financially.

There would be other landscaping and grading jobs over the next few years. The firm would grow and expand once again – this time without any outside financing. Although the equipment fleet got larger, it did not get any better in terms of quality. It was almost as though Dad had a personal fear of owning construction equipment and trucks he could be proud of. Without a doubt, having gone broke twice severely restricted his desire to go into debt on any vehicles or equipment.

1964 brought a new opportunity in the landscaping side of the business. This new line of work offered by the firm would develop into a substantial profit center for the next two decades. I know. I was a part of this operation from the beginning.

The growing, harvesting, transporting and installation of cultured sod had recently been developed as a new method of turf landscaping in the metro Twin Cities area. Cultured sod means that turf grasses are grown as an agricultural crop to be harvested and planted for lawns or athletic fields.

Going back in time, sodding was not a new idea nor was the sodding business something totally new for the firm or the area. The old Eau Claire Nursery, Inc. had done sodding all over western Wisconsin. During these past times though, the sod was harvested from farmer's pastures which was mowed just prior to harvesting the sod – that is if the cattle hadn't done the mowing previously. If left to the cattle, there would always be the "deposits" left in the turf. This "pasture sod" was cut in strips one foot wide and several inches thick. This sod had to be cut thick because the root structure of these grasses and weeds would not hold together in the rolled-up strips during transportation to the jobsite. Because of the extreme labor intensity required to produce this stuff, it was used only on the most severely sloped lawn areas or in the flow line of ditches or other areas prone to erosion. Due to the high costs involved in the process in those days, sodding was restricted to areas where there really was no other option to establish turf while preventing erosion.

"Cultured sod" changed all of the old methods and the thinking about turf grass and turf establishment. Changed too were the procedures for doing the all of the actual work involved in the sodding process. "Cultured sod" was being grown on huge fields specifically to be a harvestable crop with known purpose and usefulness. No longer a blend of field grasses and weeds, this beautiful turf crop was mowed methodically, weed treated and manicured which created a most perfect, noxious weed free turf field. The constant mowing and manicuring created thick, fibrous root mass which allowed for a thinner, lighter thickness in the harvesting process. This thinner, lighter depth of cut reduced the weight of the product for transportation purposes significantly. Additionally, the lighter weight gave greater ease of handling for both the harvesting and installation portions of the process All of these factors combined to make "cultured sod" a huge success for Kenneth R. Freitag, Inc.

 My dad had become fascinated by this booming industry on his many trips to "the Cities". He became interested enough to find out where to go and whom to talk to so that he could bring this new method of lawn building to western Wisconsin. His inquiries paid off and soon he was the only firm offering cultured sod lawns in the area. Thousands and thousands of square yards of this product were transported from the Minnesota sod fields east to his many jobsites in western Wisconsin.

When I was a sixteen-year-old high school kid, I would finish up with classes for the day and I'd drive home to change into work clothes. I'd then drive to Dad's shop, get in a truck and make the two-hundred-mile round trip to pick up loads of cultured sod several nights per week. (I made a lot of those after school trips!) By doing so, the crews had the product in Eau Claire ready to be installed when they arrived for work in the morning and didn't have to wait for the product to be delivered from Minnesota.

1967 began a new twist for the firm related to the sodding business. The Minnesota sod producer, with whom Dad had been dealing, owned and developed a number of "cultured sod" fields throughout four upper mid-western states. Unbeknown to my dad, this man had developed a cultured sod field only twenty miles west of Dad's business at Menomonie, Wisconsin. He called Dad that spring stating that he wanted Kenny to have exclusive harvesting rights to this new field. He expressed to Dad how he had come to respect and appreciate dad's good word and payment promptness. Dad thanked him but went on to say that we did not have the proper harvesting equipment and therefore probably could not do the work.

The developer expressed to Dad how he had enjoyed their business relationship with Kenny and that there was no one else whom he wanted to be in the "cultured sod" business with in Wisconsin. Dad agreed on the deal and purchased the harvesting equipment. He was in the "cultured sod" business in a bigger fashion than he had ever imagined. Now, Dad's firm now controlled harvesting, transportation and installation. The developer was paid a fee on a per acre basis for sod harvested in a prompt manner which kept him happy. This in turn, put Kenny in a business with no local competition. The "cultured sod" business was going crazy.

This new line of work, along with the continuation of the other previous endeavors, resulted in a period of substantial growth and profitability for the firm. Larger trucks were added to the fleet to handle the increasing volumes of sod to be transported. More forklifts were added to handle the loading of sod for the wholesale buyers who were now coming to the sod field from distant parts of the state. During that era, a nationwide housing boom was happening and dad's firm was in the right business at the right time!

My sixteenth, seventeenth and eighteenth summers were spent with the firm as a member of the sod crew. At the end of my eighteenth summer, I went on an extended tour which offered me both travel and adventure. I signed up to be a U.S. Navy Seabee as a heavy equipment operator/truck driver and went to Vietnam.

I had noticed a change in my dad during those summers before enlisting in the service. He no longer seemed as inspired as he had been during the time of his third rebuilding of his business. He seemed to lack the enthusiasm he always displayed during the tougher times when he had to devote himself totally to the task of starting all over again. Something had changed in him – but what?

I found out when I returned from Vietnam.

On a triangular piece of land at the intersection of U.S. Highway 12 and County Highway "T", which had formerly been a hog wallow, and not too far from the repair shop building was now constructed a large Swiss style building. This new building was his new dream – a retail landscaping and gardening store which my mother had titled Alpine Landscape Center in honor of dad's Swiss heritage.

Like his father before him, that old bloodline genetic mutation had resurfaced again. It was as if he could not stand prosperity. Without debt, with cash in the bank, he came to lack the motivation, the drive, the will to push his business ahead. Other than this newfound sodding niche, he had become lethargic – lacked the aggressiveness – no longer had that "go-get-em" hunger for business that he had in the past. It seemed as though he became indifferent, uninterested in the success or failure of the firm. He was just too financially comfortable.

Evidently, he craved the potential peril, the danger of a do-or-die financial load with the precarious financial predicament that goes along with huge debt. In order that this new Swiss style building project and the dream of a retail landscaping and gardening store could come into being, once again, he had plunged deep in debt.

This new huge debt load caused him to be motivated to a level similar to when he had the machinery debt from the past. His workaholism reached a level unseen since the road contracting era. He spent more and more time with his business and less and less time with his family. He was so immersed in his business now that he was back in debt in a huge way that, his business became his hobby, his social life, his recreation, his total focus, his everything.

Dad drove his work crews, his staff, his family and himself to new levels of greater performance. It was as if this massive debt caused him to acquire new energies to direct the firm's attack on this new financial burden. He became unrelenting in this renewed drive to increase sales, do more work, attain more revenue and increase profitability. He was completely obsessed with his business. This obsession became so all-encompassing that he degenerated to the point where he could converse on nothing other than his business. Since business was his total realm of interest and involvement, nothing else seemed to be of any interest to him at all.

He drove his family in that business direction along with him. Mother worked in the office doing bookkeeping and payrolls. My sister worked in the retail store in her spare time when not attending high school. I worked the sodding end of the business with up to twenty employees under my direction while attempting to be a college student. We worked together as a team to overcome the debt load which my dad had taken on for the firm. It worked.

Our debt load was continually being downsized. The firm became financially healthy enough to be able to once again trade off older equipment and upgrade the fleet. As the debt load was paid down, the banker came to love us. They even solicited our business. All of the local banks were calling our firm two and three times per year to persuade us to become their clients. Bankers must talk to one-another, at least in Eau Claire, Wisconsin.

As the firm grew and expanded, so did the territory we worked. We even began to cross state borders for projects.

The 1977 season had come to a very profitable end. In late October, dad purchased two dump trucks and a brand-new front-end-loader in anticipation of a very promising 1978 season. The firm had taken on some short-term debt to finance the purchase of this equipment.

One evening in early November, when dad was in the office working late as usual, he received a phone call which would change our financial situation in a way unforeseen when the equipment purchases were made.

The sod field developer called to tell dad that he had an urgent need for cash to finance a real-estate deal that he was working on at the time. Because of his need for the cash, the developer *told* Dad that, he Kenny, *was going to buy him out of his Menomonie, Wisconsin, sod farm operations.* Dad shared with the developer that he had just purchased this equipment and that he didn't think the bank would go along with him on borrowing additional funds with which to make this deal happen. The developer, being a seasoned businessman, ignored what Dad had just shared with him concerning our firm's finances. He told Dad to bring me with him (he knew I handled the sod operations) and come to his office in Minnesota to discuss the matter.

I was working in the office that evening as well. When Dad hung up the phone, he was very obviously shaken. He was being forced into a situation not of his own making and for which he was completely unprepared. The situation was this; *either buy the sod farm at a price dictated by the developer and remain in control of the "cultured sod" business in western Wisconsin or not buy the sod field and lose control of a very highly profitable portion of the firm's business.*

What to do?

The next morning dad called our banker to explain this new development in the sod business as it related to the firm. He went on to explain how the inability to purchase the sod farm would have an adverse effect on our total sales revenue as well as our end-of-the-year bottom line. Not knowing what the developer had in mind for a sale price for the farm, Dad asked the banker to go along with making a loan to the firm of up to a purchase price of $150,000.00 for the sod farm. This would be an even larger loan than he had taken on to build the landscape and garden center building.

The banker told Dad to go to the meeting and, as he put it, "Write the check. We'll cover it." Armed only with the promised commitment from the banker, Dad and I went to the meeting.

Dad had estimated the value of the as yet unharvested acreage of the sod crop along with the property value to determine what he figured the developer would be the asking price for the sod farm. On our drive to the developer's office, we discussed what we thought would take place at the meeting. We agreed that this would be a rather simple deal. As he had shared with the banker, we had basically two options; 1.) either accept the price, terms and conditions, or, 2.) if the price was too high for us to handle, walk away from the deal and be out of the sod harvesting business. Dad felt quite certain of the price, the terms and conditions and was prepared to write a check for the full amount at $150,000.00. If the developer wanted more than what Dad had estimated, we would be out of the sod harvesting business other than owning sod harvesting equipment which would be of no value to us if we had no sod to harvest.

The meeting began with a luncheon, small talk, reminiscing and business in general. I was a silent spectator. Dad was noticeably nervous. The developer was quite aware of Dad's nervousness too. The only way Dad's nervousness could have been more obvious was if he had had a big sign around his neck reading "I'M A NERVOUS WRECK" in big bold letters. After the luncheon, we went back to the developer's office to listen to the deal.

Dad and I followed the developer back into his spacious office. One wall was lined with four drawer file cabinets. He pulled open one drawer filled with portfolios, each one of his property holdings. He thumbed his way through the files until, "Yes, here it is – Menomonie, Wisconsin." He pulled the file and laid it on his desk. Nerves were frayed on our side of the desk!

He began again. "Well, Kenny, I'm going to look at that farm this way. I'll forget the fact that there is a lot of prime turf grass on it. I'll basically forget that I increased the value of the property since I purchased it. I just want to get my cash out of that parcel so I can make this other investment which has tremendous potential for my real estate portfolio. You have been an excellent tenant of my property and over time, I've come to consider you a friend." (I suppose it was very clear that both Dad and I were sweating at this point. There was nothing else we could do and there definitely was no way to hide our uneasiness.) He went on again. "So, here's the deal – a one-time-offer – today only. I'll just pretend there is no sod on the property and you will be buying the farm as if it were raw land only. I want $100,00.00 cash by the end of the week so I can do my other deal. I'll leave the room so you guys can talk this over I'll be back in ten minutes."

He rose from behind his desk. Dad rose and offered his hand and said, "That won't be necessary, we have a deal."

"I'll have my lawyers draw up the contract and get the stuff to you. I need to move on this fast. By the way, Kenny, could I have a dip of your Copenhagen?" Both men smiled as the snuff was dipped (myself not included, though I was offered a pinch).

The developer asked, "Did my price come as a surprise to you?" as a few kernels of snuff fell from his lower lip.

It was one of Dad's finer moments when he replied, "Well, as you know, you sort of had me "over-the-barrel." I really had no choice but to say "yes" to whatever price you named. Just for your own peace of mind, I was prepared to go to $150,000.00 but no more."

Dad smiled and so did the developer. He said, "No Kenny, you have always been honest with me since we started. You never tried to cheat me out of a nickel. I just can't find guys like you anymore. Because you've always been right with me, this was my way of being right with you."

Dad wrote the $100,000.00 check right there in the developer's office and handed it to him. They shook hands once again and we left for home.

WOW!

Dad had just purchased the sod farm for 2/3 of what he had been prepared to spend. He didn't even attempt to do any negotiations given the offered price. I got to witness two businessmen who respected one-another completely act as gentlemen towards each other on a business deal. It was a beautiful thing to observe. I don't know if you'd see such a thing anymore.

Now, although heavily in debt once again, we were in the sod business and in total control like never before.

For the next several years, there would be heightened business activities for the firm. The debt load was being constantly lowered and the equipment fleet was expanded and upgraded and improved.

1980 began as any other season did, but by early July of that year, sales and operations were as slow as they had ever been for the past decade. Only five employees remained on the payroll and they were mostly doing repairs and maintenance on the vehicles and equipment. This situation was about to change in a spectacular fashion.

Mother had booked a flight for her and Dad to visit Switzerland and Germany that summer in mid-July. Dad had specified that the trip be in July since it was normally a slow month for the business every year. Given the extremely slow conditions this year, even the most serious cases of workaholics could pull themselves away from a business that was sputtering along at best. Their flight was to leave on the morning of July 16, 1980.

During the night of the 15 of July, a destructive wind storm with gale-force winds of up to 115 MPH hit western Wisconsin. Many buildings were wrecked. About 1/3 of the trees in town were either broken off or up-rooted. The city was a spectacular mess. Many of the streets were impassable because of fallen trees and debris. Numerous homes were ruined or, at least damaged, in one way or another. The entire city was without electrical power for five days And, those with power restored in five days were the lucky ones. In many areas the power was first restored in two weeks or so after the storm. What a disaster!

Dad knew this storm and the resulting damage it had caused offered potential work for the company on a grand scale. Leaving that morning of July 16 was torture for him. He would have gladly given up his ticket to go to Europe. Reluctantly, he left town but my mother had to nearly drag him away from the devastated town.

Sensing the potential that night myself, I called two trusted employees. I asked them each to be at the two businesses which sold chainsaws at 5:30 a.m. and buy as many chainsaws as they could carry out the door. Those six new chainsaws along with the six that we already owned really put us in the disaster cleanup business.

From a near business drought, suddenly we had business like never before. We recalled every crew member whom we had just recently laid off and then hired more. At one time during this period, we had six crew chiefs and over 100 other employees, many of the latter whom I never even knew. Every piece of equipment and every vehicle we owned was at work cleaning up the mess.

My sister Janet and her staff at the store were taking the calls from people in need of our services. The store staff was scheduling many of the crew activities and meeting with the crew chiefs to dispatch the workload. I was meeting with customers to look at the work to determine which piece of equipment or vehicle would be needed on each job. Additionally, I checked on jobsite progress for scheduling purposes. The company and its crews were running like a finely tuned Swiss watch.

The City of Eau Claire hired our firm to supply several of our front-end-loaders to remove downed trees from the city streets. Our dump trucks, the ones we could spare, were hired by the city to haul the downed trees and debris to disposal sites. We dispatched machines, trucks and power tools to a housing development which was particularly hard hit on the west side of town. Our crews worked seven days a week and this crazy pace was maintained for over two months. Fourteen to sixteen-hour days were not uncommon during those first few weeks of the cleanup operation. Once the city was opened up so that the streets were once again drivable, we cut our workdays back to ten to twelve hours per day.

The money rolled in. I mean, THE MONEY ROLLED IN! I had secured a line of credit with the banker to cover the initial payrolls for this unprecedented number of employees. As it turned out, we never had to borrow a cent to meet payroll. Customers were so grateful for the service and the work performed by the firm and its employees that they paid for the work upon completion. These early-on-the-list private home owners carried the day until the larger firms and the city began to send their money to the firm. This is the sort of business frenzy which all businesspeople dream of.

When our parents returned from their European trip, they could not believe all that was going on with the business. Crew members they had never met, business activity on a level they had never seen, vehicles coming and going at all hours of the day and night. But most importantly, a checkbook with a six-figure balance and all of the bills paid.

At this point, and for the first time ever in his life, Dad began to question a notion he had long held about his children. He was no longer certain that his children had been dropped head-first onto the birthing room floor. He could actually see that they had some slight hope of making it in the world of business. This revelation did not come easy for him, but looking at the business activity and the checkbook he was forced to come to grips with it. The downside of Dad's return from the trip was that he wanted to take over he operations of the firm. After all, he had been the "top dog", the "big cheese", the "head honcho" and the firm was his. My sister and I had things well under control and it was the two of us who had the contacts, knew what to do and why and when to do things. So, in a way, Dad's attempt at taking over operations had to be thwarted by my sister and I which was tough.

By the time the parents returned home, besides the 75 people doing disaster cleanup work, we had a few equipment operators working on some preliminaries on a golf course construction project at our neighbor's farm. Dad had been meeting with these neighbors to talk about this job for over a year. While the parents were in Europe, the financing for the project came through. Not wanting to lose the job to others, I moved equipment on the jobsite a few days before the parents returned to the United States. I'm glad I got the golf course job started when I did.

Since Janet and I had the day-to-day cleanup operations well under control, we needed to get Dad "out of our hair". After all, he had no idea of the agreements we had made and didn't know our contacts. We asked him to go run the operations on the golf course construction project and let us continue doing what we knew how to do. We had things under control and he needed to understand that. So, Dad was kept busy with the golf course project and that was good for him but especially for my sister and myself.

At this same time, one of the area's largest housing developers with whom our firm had been doing a lot of work over the past decade received a H.U.D. housing contract to build eleven low-income housing buildings. I had submitted a bid to them for the basement excavation and backfill, the site grading together with all the lawn work and shrubbery installation and I was their low bidder. So, we had this job to do now as well.

Generally, business people are supposed to complain about business, or the level of business or the profitability of the business or, complain about something or everything or, just complain. We were unable to say anything negative about our business. We were not swamped with business, we were BURIED! It was wonderful! It was unbelievable! It was business euphoria! This was business as it can only be dreamt about.

To merely state that our firm had a banner year would be to do our efforts a gross injustice. We had outperformed the best of the past 50 years in the company's history by over 40% in both sale's revenue and profitability. Couple that with new machinery purchases for cash and a substantially reduced debt load and you have quite a record year indeed. I guess the only negative comment made about the year was when I told Dad we had just won the contract on the H.U.D. housing project and he commented, "Well, isn't that just great! We have more work than we can possibly handle now and then you have to go land another big one."

I'll take that kind of complaint any day!

1981 was a similar kind of business season. Even without a big windstorm, we did exceptionally well.

In September Dad sensed something about the future business cycle which he was somehow very good at forecasting. I never did figure out how he knew this, but he claimed that the economy would be poor for the next several years. He could "just feel it." We were busy enough at the time and I had never experienced a business "downturn". The idea of such a thing happening and his forecast of such a calamity was nearly impossible for me to grasp. Dad was so convinced of his premonition that he jumped at a very strange opportunity which came about in a most peculiar fashion.

The son of one of Dad's former mechanics from his time as a road building contractor had taken a job as a "roughneck" in the oil patch around Williston, North Dakota. It seemed that the oilfield people really liked the hustle, the work ethic of upper-mid-westerners. One such crew chief noticed this young fellow from Wisconsin on his crew and asked the young man if he knew of any Wisconsin earthmoving contractors who would be willing to set up an operation out in the Williston Basin. This would be to do "location work" -site grading of the area upon which the drilling rigs are set up along with dikes for sludge pits for the drilling waste plus the related road work for drilling site access, etc. This young man called his father back in Wisconsin with questions about area earthmovers and the "roughneck's" father called his former employer, my dad. After exchanging information, my dad called an oilfield consultant in Williston. He made an appointment to meet with him to talk over the work and job requirements for machinery and manpower.

That fall, Dad and I took the trip to the Williston Basin. Together we spent several days looking at the area and the work related to oil field earthmoving construction. We met and talked with several area consultants and other "oil patch" people to check things out and gather as much information as possible while in the area.

On the trip back to Wisconsin, I noticed Dad was quite negative about the prospects of this oilfield work even though he "knew" that our next season at home was going to be bad in the business sense. This was the first time that I had ever seen him in such a negative mood about future business opportunities. The only things he talked about on our trip home were the negative things – all of the downside of the work we had just looked at.

What was wrong with him? Why all of this negativism? Was it his age? The distance from home? Entering a new type of business? What was the problem?

Within two months of the trip, Dad was hospitalized with colon cancer. He never came home from the hospital. He died on Thanksgiving Day, 1981. He was not quite two months past his 67th birthday

My father's funeral was a large event. Many of his former employees, business associates, suppliers, customers and even a number of competitors were there to pay their last respects. People even showed up at the wake from several states, standing in line to share their condolences.

Looking back on that day now, I am still overwhelmed with the turnout of all who came to his funeral that day. The mourners had not gathered to give a big "send-off" to a great businessman. By most standards, his level of success had been moderate at best. They were not there because of his prestige or social standing in the community. Dad's civic devotion was not what brought them there either. Certainly, these folks were not there to comfort a grieving family. Many of those present did not recognize my mother, my sister or myself. These attendees had to introduce themselves and inform us of their reason for being there, or in many cases, to explain their business relationship with Dad.

If my father was really not a huge business success or a man of great prestige or high position within the community and the mourners were really not there to comfort the family whom many didn't even know, what was it that brought the big turnout to Dad's funeral?

I believe now, and I always will, that it was respect in respect's purest form which brought that many people together to pay their last respects to my father. He left this world and his beloved world of business a winner. He had come to be recognized as a dominant force in his chosen field within the geographic area in which he operated his business. He had gone out at the top of his form. These attendees had gathered at my father's funeral to pay tribute to a champion, a warrior, who had left the field of battle victorious.

But more importantly, my father was the living personification of perseverance. He had gone BROKE not once but twice. That was true. He never gave up, he never quit and never, ever stopped trying. He overcame all of the setbacks he had experienced in his long business career. When he left us, he had won against all of the adversities of his past to triumph in that war zone known as American Small Business.

PART III - NEW LEADERSHIP AND NEW DIRECTION

DOWNTURN WITH A SAFETY NET

My sister and I had to fill the leadership void after dad's death. There was no one else to take charge. Although we had had some experience in the management of the business, we were not really ready to take over day-to-day operations in the manner we were now finding ourselves. As is all too often the case in a small business dominated by one strong willed individual such as our father, he never let go of the top spot in the organization. He couldn't. It is the way guys like him are made. We had little choice, my sister and I. We would have to operate the business whether we were ready to do so or not.

Although our business had made some good profits in the last several years, we were by no means debt free. There were still many creditors – both short term and long term. Dad's insurance policy served only to bolster our liquidity.

Dad's predictions prior to his death were correct about the upcoming season. There was a tremendous downturn in business activity in our area. Interest rates on new home construction climbed to over 20% in early 1982. As a result, the housing industry – our primary market – took a nose dive. It made no sense to try to sell the business. We could not get a reasonable return on our investment since all buyers would know that the main market served by the business had all but collapsed. We knew it would be foolish to try to sell the business given the present business climate.

As the 1982 season began to develop, by mid- March both my sister and I could see that the normal level of business was not going to happen that year. One of the main problems, of course, was that the namesake of the business was no longer present. There are always those customers who wish to deal only with the individual whose name appears on the door and the letterhead. How many times during that first season after my father's death was it we had to explain that Kenny was no longer among the living? The news was a real shocker to many.

Just as he had warned me, the business climate that year developed as he said it would. He had told me of years in which there was little or nothing to be done in our line of work. Worse, there was absolutely nothing that could be done to change this economically driven phenomenon. Prices could be slashed, marketing levels could be increased, sales efforts expanded. Yet when the market does not exist, or at best, only a very diminished market is all that there is left to deal with, there is simply nothing a small businessperson can do to change this situation. This is exactly how the 1982 season took shape. Even having been warned of the possibility of a business climate of this nature by Dad, my sister and I entered the season in total and complete disbelief. Since graduating from college and joining the firm full time, we had always been involved in an "up" market. It was increase – not decrease - I was used to in business activity. The 1982 season was a foreign experience for my sister and I and we no longer had the benefit of our father's experience to guide us through this calamity we had never experienced.

How was it that he could see this economic downturn? How was it that the accuracy of his prediction would result in the sort of business year just as he said it would?

Having been through this situation before in his many years in business, on out trip back from Williston, he shared with me, "There will come a time when you go to the shop just like you have become used to each morning. You will open the garage door on the shop and look out at the lineup of the trucks and machinery. The crew will be there, but there is nothing for the crew nor the trucks nor the machinery to work on. There are no projects. There is no work." How very correct he was about such a situation. I remembered that prediction one morning early in the season when just such a scenario took place at the shop.

All that could be done, he told me, was to visit your good old trusted customers with whom you had done business for years, to see if they had anything going that you might offer to bid. Trying this, I was told that they had nothing going either at the time and that they would let me know when something, anything developed. They were not just saying this to try to get rid of me. They were sincere. There really was nothing happening in the area. It was a dismal beginning to the season without my tutor.

Dad's most visionary prophesy was the one where he had said, "There will be many times after I am no longer with you that you will wish there was a way to talk to me for just a minute or so to help you through a problem you are having. My experience could be of great value to you, yet you will have to make decisions without the benefit of what I have learned in my lifetime. How do I know this? That answer lies in how many times I wished I could have talked to my father after he was gone. Now I know all of this sounds very strange to you, but just remember I told you this." How many times during that 1982 season did I remember these words and remember them well?

During the spring of 1982, we experienced a brief spurt of activity. By the end of May, everything went dead. We had no choice other than to lay off employees, park equipment and cut back on everything. Since my discharge from the military and my involvement with the firm, I had never seen anything like this before.

By mid-summer we were down to a three to four-man crew. A job was sold one day and the crew was dispatched to do the work the next day. We were literally running a hand-to-mouth operation.

A service friend of mine from Houston, Texas, called one day and shared stories about how poorly things were going for his business that season. Tom was in business with his father and they were large scale earthmoving contractors. He told of their inability to secure any contracts in the Houston area. This had forced him to search for projects outside the normal area of operations for their firm. They had contracted for a project in the Oklahoma City, Oklahoma, area. He asked if I had any large dump trucks that were not too busy. I had one four axle dump truck. I jumped at the chance to put a driver and a vehicle to work even if it was 1000 miles from home. The job was supposed to last several months and this sounded good to me. I was sick of looking at that truck just sitting there in the lineup every morning. Oklahoma City or not, it was a job and I took it. That deal was about the highlight of that dismal season and there was nothing that could be done about that. It's good to have friends.

On the good news front, Dad's insurance policy death benefit allowed us to "stay afloat" financially and keep our payments current at the bank. So, despite the turndown in the economy, at that time in our business history, we did have a safety net. Without that safety net we probably would have gone broke during that disastrous business season of 1982.

EARLY SUCCESSES

Though 1983 was basically a repeat of 1982, the 1984 season started to show signs of improvement for our business. I had successfully negotiated several larger grading and sitework jobs which allowed us to put our fleet of equipment back to work. We were able to recall all of our laid-off employees after two terrible years back-to-back. After two years of virtual nothingness, being back in business in the spring of 1984 certainly felt great.

As the season developed, more work kept coming our way. The improved economy helped with retail sales at the landscape/garden center store operations as well as the upswing in the earthmoving side of the business. Both my sister and I were enjoying a rewarding and challenging season and we were both grateful to see things working well for our firm once again.

Our neighbors, for whom dad had built the golf course in his final year, wanted to add nine holes to their nine-hole golf course. Given the high interest rates at the time, they just couldn't get enough play on a nine-hole golf course to get out from under their debt load. They were "barely keeping their head above water". Their bank would not finance the additional work. I offered to do the work and hold the billing (in other words, finance the construction project) until they were generating enough revenue to off our firm. We agreed to a price for the work and we commenced construction. We were back in the golf course construction business. We finished 1984 showing a small profit.

Fiscally, 1985 was a repeat of 1984 for our firm. We had no golf course work but we did have other larger grading and landscaping projects which allowed us to top our breakeven point. During the fall of 1985, the workload fell off drastically. We completed all of the scheduled work prior to the November "freeze up, closing out the year with no backlog for the upcoming 1986 season.

During September 1985, I noticed a project which was of interest to me in one of the trade publications. The project was a long distance from our normal area of operations. Knowing we had nothing for the upcoming season, I decided to take a look at this job. It could be said that this was an act of desperation. Having no work for the coming year, I sent for a set of plans, "specs" and bidding documents.

This project called for the construction of a nine-hole golf course addition at the K.I. Sawyer Air Force Base in the upper peninsula of the State of Michigan. The Air Force Base was located 30 miles south of Marquette, Michigan, about 350 miles from our place of business. I felt comfortable about my knowledge of golf course construction since I had done two projects of a similar nature and scope for our neighbors. After receiving the plans, I decided to take a look at the project site.

I drove up in early October. I found the base and once inside located the contracting office. Finding the individual in charge of the golf course construction project, I introduced myself and explained I was there to look over the proposed project site. I was given a base map and directions from the contracting office to the existing nine-hole golf course. After finding the golf course, I met with the superintendent who took me for a tour of the of the proposed construction site. I knew this was the job for me. The soil was all sand and the area was already cleared of trees and brush. The project was simply grading, seeding and irrigation system installation. I would not need a big crew nor would I need much equipment to do the job. The job was straight forward and rather simple. I decided to "take a shot" at this one. The bids were due in December.

Back at home, I spent many hours on the phone seeking material prices from local Michigan contractors and suppliers. I did my calculations, my figuring, my educated guessing and all the other factors that enter into the bidding process. At the end of all that, I felt good about my bid price. I filled in the bid sheet, sealed it in an envelope, marked it per federal regulation and took it to the post office. I sent the bid to the K.I. Sawyer Air Force Base Contracting Office via Express Mail Guaranteed Overnight Delivery. I could not attend the bid letting personally as I had other matters to attend to at the time.

One day after the scheduled sealed bid opening, I called the contracting officer to find out the bid results. I introduced myself over the phone and asked what the bid results were for the golf course project. He asked me who I was and what firm I was with and what the project bid results had to do with me or my firm. I identified myself as the president of our firm and said that I was a bidder on the golf course project. I told him I had driven up to the base to look over the job and that I had even stopped in his office to introduce myself. Oh yes, he did remember me but wondered why I hadn't submitted a bid on the project. He informed me that his office had not received a bid from our firm prior to the bid opening deadline. I couldn't believe it. My bid had arrived late and, therefore, was never opened! Federal procurement regulations stipulate that bids which are not received prior to the scheduled date and time for bid opening will not be opened.

I asked if a bid tabulation sheet would be sent out to the bidders. He said that normally a bid tabulation sheet would be sent out but only to those firms who had submitted an opened bid for the project. I was not considered a bidder since my bid arrived late, and by rule, it was never opened. I explained that I just wanted to see how competitive my bid had been in relation to the other bidders. He said he could not help me. I was crushed!

Two weeks later, I received a letter from the K.I. Sawyer Air Force Base Contracting Office informing me that all of the previous bids for the golf course expansion project had been rejected. The project was going to be re-bid in January of 1986.

Later, I found out the details about the first round of bidding. Base contracting had received only two bids (other than my disqualified one). One was from a local area landscaping contractor who had absolutely no experience in golf course construction what-so-ever. The other was from a Virginia firm. While my resume sheet was rather weak, at that time, at least I could establish that our firm had actually done golf course construction, though on a limited basis. When I had bid the project for the first time, I was aware of the pre-qualification requirements concerning golf course construction experience. I knew we didn't fully meet the experience requirement. Though our firm was a few holes short of the pre-qualification requirement, I decided to submit a bid on the project anyway.

The day after receiving the letter, I got a phone call from the contracting officer requesting information about our firm's history in the golf course construction business. I answered all of his questions about our previous golf course experience. I offered to send him a copy of our resume which contained contact information from our previous clients. He asked me to send it out as soon as possible. I sent the information out that day but wondered why there was such urgency about this information.

Upon receipt of the second set of plans, "specs" and bidding documents for the re-bidding of the project, I found out the reason why the contracting officer had to have the requested information on our firm ASAP. The contracting officer had made some notes concerning our first meeting which he must have put in the project file. Because of that initial meeting, and those notes he had kept, he knew that I had discussed with him that I didn't fully meet the pre-qualification requirements, but that I did have golf course construction experience. Based on the resume I sent him, the pre-qualifications were *re-written* to make our firm eligible as a qualified bidder!

I was pleased to have a second opportunity to bid on this project. I just might have a good chance of winning this bid. But this time I made up my mind that I would definitely be present at the bid opening in person.

I headed up to the base a couple of days before the January bid date. On my way to the job, I stopped in Park Falls, Wisconsin, at the St. Croix Fishing Rod Manufacturing Company. Here I purchased a brand-new fishing rod and reel. I figured that if I did not win this job at the Air Force Base, I might just spend a little more time fishing that summer. Other than this project, prospects were looking quite slim in and around my local territory.

The winter months in Marquette, Michigan, on Lake Superior's southern shore must be experienced to be believable. On average, Michigan's upper peninsula receives 240 inches (yup, that's right, 20 feet) of snowfall during the winter months. Streets become tunnel-like rat mazes with huge mounds of snow 10 -15 feet high that border all the streets and parking lots alike. In many cases, you need to know where businesses and certain buildings are located because you cannot see these things from the snowbank enshrouded streets. As a Wisconsin resident, I expect snow in the winter, but I have never experienced anything like Marquette, Michigan!

This time I actually met with local contractors and suppliers face to face to get prices for the project. So, they actually came to know me as I got to meet with and know them. I could not help but thinking of my dad as I sat in the hotel room figuring the final bid price for the project. I went over everything – every part of the job seven times. I was still taking price quotations over the phone and figuring and re-figuring quantities until late at night. I was checking and re-checking my figures in between phone calls, trying to be as competitive as possible but without cutting my own throat. Welcome to the wonderful world of contracting.

The day of the bid opening arrived. I knew I was as ready as I could be. I drove out to the Air Force Base arriving over an hour before the bids were to be opened and read.

During the time prior to the bid opening, I talked with the contracting officer about the previous bid. I knew that he was limited in the scope of answers he could share with me, so I tried not to ask questions which would put him in an uncomfortable situation. I asked him if he could tell me why the original bids had been rejected. He began by answering that three bids had been received, one of which (mine) could not be opened because it arrived late and therefore, was not a legal bid. Of the other two, he went on (here is where I found out the details of the first round of bidding.) one of the bidders had no golf course construction experience at all and the other bidder with a voluminous resume offered a bid price so far over budget that that firm's bid had to be rejected. Since base personnel really wanted the golf course addition, it was decided to try rebidding the project. His answers made it clear to me why he had requested the background information on our firm and our experience. I thanked him for sharing the information.

It was bid opening time – 2:00 p.m. eastern standard time (1400 hours – military time). I'm certain that I was visibly nervous. This was the highest dollar amount bid our firm had ever submitted in the firm's nearly 60-year history. My bid price for the project was right around one half million dollars! There were only two sealed bid envelopes on the table – mine and one from a golf course construction firm from out on the east coast. I guessed this to be the firm whose bid was rejected on the first round of bidding due to being way over budget.

Their bid was opened first. Way higher than mine – just under three quarters of a million dollars! I knew right then that I had won! However, I had left a lot "on the table" - nearly a quarter million dollars! That was a discomforting thing to think about on my 350-mile drive back home. As is done in the bidding process, after my bid was opened, my firm was termed the "apparent low bidder". This did not guarantee that my firm would be awarded the contract. It only notes that on the day of the reading of the bids, my firm was the low bidder. After bids are opened and read, all documents must be checked for improprieties, mathematical errors, omissions and flaws. The bid bond needs to be included. If all is in order on the bidding documents and the offered contract price is within budgeted limits, a contract will be awarded.

The next 45 days seemed an eternity for this young contractor wanting and very badly needing this work. Apparent low bidder is one thing, and having a contract is quite another.

The contract documents finally arrived (in quadruplicate, of course – this is a government contract). I signed and executed the documents in the contract, secured the performance bonding and prepared all the other paperwork involved in the contracting game. I was very thorough and diligent filling out all the forms to satisfy the paperwork requirements, after all, I was dealing with government bureaucrats. I had just landed the largest contract in our firm's history.

As mid-March arrived, I received an invitation to bid on 12-hole golf course construction project to build 9 new holes and remodel 3 existing holes in Eagle River, Wisconsin. We were beginning to move equipment to the Air Force Base job at this time and our route to that job took us right through Eagle River. I decided to pick up a set of plans and bidding documents for this project at the Eagle River City Hall on one of the trips north to K.I. Sawyer Air Force Base. On that trip, besides picking up the plans and "specs", I stopped to talk to the local contractor who was doing the clearing on the site under separate contract. We talked about working on this project together. He quoted material prices and hourly equipment rates. I brought all of this information back to my office for study, worked over the plans and "specs" to determine quantities of materials needed and began the bidding process all over again.

Because of my experience on the first bid at the Air Force Base, I personally attended the bid opening at Eagle River. When the bids were read, my firm was read as the "apparent low bidder". That project made it two huge jobs for my firm – each one individually twice the size or better than any previous single project in the company's history.

These new contract documents arrived in 30 days. We were really doing business on a scale never before realized in our firm's history.

With over a million dollars of work under contract, business seemed like a dream. A local site grading project worth over a quarter of a million came in mid-April. All sorts of landscaping projects and various other jobs kept pouring in at a pace we had never seen before. We were hiring more people, adding equipment to the fleet, even renting additional equipment beyond that which we purchased. It was WILD!

In August we contracted for yet another golf course project in the Milwaukee area which made 1986 a year of unprecedented growth and profitability for our firm. When our fiscal year was ended, we showed six times the sales of any previous year in company history. Profitability was at a level we had never imagined. We awarded bonuses to our crew leaders and both my sister and I took bonuses ourselves. As the construction season came to a close, I was bidding on a golf course construction project over in the metro-Detroit area. Everything was looking up for our firm.

Back in 1983 my wife and I purchased a lakeshore lot on Lake Superior in northern Minnesota near the beautiful little town of Grans

Marais. We paid off the land contract on the property during the wild business season of 1986. We had always dreamed of a rustic log cabin on our lakeshore lot. Believing that the previous season was going to be a trend for our firm, my wife and I decided to use my bonus funds from the company along with a sizable loan to make our dream come true.

We met with a local custom log cabin builder in November of 1986. We drew up a rough floor plan of what we wanted on the back of a placemat at a local restaurant. I informed the builder that I wasn't interested in a *toothpick* cabin. I wanted a *log* cabin built using huge diameter logs.

The log builder had these plans refined. The cabin, though small, was to have all the features we had been dreaming of over the years- huge stone fire place, vaulted ceilings, a spiral staircase leading to two bedrooms on the upper floor and big windows offering great views of the largest body of fresh water in the world. We were assured all of these features would be included in the price. We met again, negotiated a price and signed a contract to have our dream cabin constructed. This cabin would be our dream come true. We were making it happen several years before we ever thought we could, but why not? Business was great and certainly it was going to get even better.

Back at the business, during the 1986-87 winter months, we upgraded our computer system and built three new buildings for of equipment and retail store inventory storage. The crew was kept busy repairing, cleaning and painting our equipment fleet. We added a few pieces of equipment in anticipation of continuing the crazy growth we had just experienced.

What we had anticipated was not to be. I was not successful on my bid for the work in the Detroit area. I bid on a number of other golf course construction projects that winter and into the spring months of 1987. Unfortunately, I never received a contract on any of the work bid.

In the spring of 1987, I was successful in contracting more local site grading projects. In addition, we had work yet to complete on two of the three golf course contracts from the previous year. Local work seemed to be coming our way. That was a good thing given my dismal showing in golf course contract bidding.

By mid-July, we were nearly out of work. We had to lay off personnel. In early September, I was successful in negotiating – not bidding – a contract for a nine-hole golf course construction project at Deerwood, Minnesota. The startup of this project allowed us to call back many of our people who were unemployed at the time. We closed out the work season with this project at Deerwood. Winter weather conditions forced us to quit the project for the season. At least we knew we would have work to do the following season.

While working at Deerwood late that fall, I was invited to attend a meeting at Lutsen, Minnesota, concerning a proposed golf course near the area's local ski resort. This project had been written about in the little local newspaper a few times that summer. Lutsen is just 17 miles southwest of our cabin at Grand Marais, Minnesota, along Lake Superior's North Shore so I was well acquainted with the area.

Prior to this invitation to the meeting that fall of 1987, the resort owner invited me to a private meeting in mid-summer. It was just him and I. After hearing about the project, I had written to him expressing my interest in the project along with making him aware of my background in the golf course construction business. He took me out on the proposed site to "walk the land" and discuss the project's current state of progress. It was this mid-summer meeting, I believe, that was instrumental in my being invited to the golf course steering committee meeting in the late fall of 1987.

WOW! What a meeting!

The golf course steering committee consisted of 12-15 area resort owners who wanted to make this project happen to increase their lodging and restaurant businesses. The resort owner whom I had met with was there, of course. I was an unknown at the meeting. Many of those gathered kept looking quizzically at me and one other guy at the meeting, whom I guessed they didn't know either. But nobody asked any questions.

The mystery of the other unknown's identity was solved right away when the meeting began. He was introduced by the committee chairman, as a representative of a world-famous golf course design firm. He was there to make a presentation to the group. I'm thinking to myself, if these committee members are thinking of building a golf course on this level, what the hell am I doing here?

I was not introduced and that was OK with me.

At the direction of the chairman, the entire group, myself included, left the conference room to "walk the land" including this "big leaguer" golf designer representative. The group spent a couple of hours in the forest "walking the land" and looking over some the most spectacular scenery to be found in the upper mid-west. We viewed the Poplar River cascading down through a mountain gorge and over a waterfall as it rushes to join Lake Superior. All the way through the tour of the proposed golf course site, the roaring river could be heard as the water's furious flow crashed through the boulder strewn streambed. If it wasn't the Poplar River you were looking at, it was the majesty of Lake Superior or the ski slopes of the mountains. Any golf course architect, designer or builder would drool over this project site just because of its natural beauty.

Once again, after the site tour, when the meeting reconvened in the conference room, I was unsure of why I had been invited to attend this meeting. There was some cordial small talk among the committee members then…

The representative of the world-famous golf course designer rose and began to speak as he handed out sales brochures to all present, even me. The brochures were exquisite with gorgeous pictures of some spectacular, stunning golf holes the firm had done around the world. There was an expansive list of projects from all over the world. Many of the golf courses on the list were world-renowned. Then too, a lot of these fabulous golf courses listed have been the host site for championship level tournaments played by the Professional Golf Association circuit on television.

So, here with the brochures and the list was *the* representative of this formidable world-wide-recognized force in the golf course design business. After handing out all of this literature, he began to relate to the assemblage how his boss was a close personal friend of Mrs. Aquino, the recently elected President of The Philippines and how he had designed a golf course for her. He went on to speak about recent work in Egypt. For the highlight of the presentation, the presenter spoke of the recently completed golf course design in the metro-Twin Cities area and how this new course was receiving rave reviews in all of the golf course related media – magazines, trade journals and, of course, television. I and all others present listened in awe to this marvelous presentation. Certainly, if his professional sales ability, the beautiful brochures, the extensive list of name-recognizable golf courses, his impressive list of global involvement in the golf course design business didn't convince those present of their need to do business with his organization, certainly the "name dropping" would get the sales job done. MY GOD! WHAT A PRESENTATION! Talk about impressive! I was not only impressed with his sales presentation, I was blown away!

Then came the hammer!

His organization would design the golf course at Lutsen, Minnesota, and the *principal* of his organization would be on the jobsite personally several times during the actual construction process. Having been designed by this world-famous super-star designer, this new golf course at Lutsen would carry the very same, very significant, much sought after name brand recognition and prestige as did all of his other world-wide projects. The committee could hire whomever they wanted to do the clearing of the forest and even do the basic earthmoving required. However, all of the finish grading, shaping and contouring would be done by personnel from their organization at an additional fee over and above the design and layout fees. That was how things were done by this organization if you wanted to be able to say that yours was a golf course designed and built by this world-famous golf course designer of international acclaim – period. Who could blame a world-renowned designer for wanting complete control of the project if his name was to be on it? He had a world-wide reputation for doing world-class work. It was mandatory for him to maintain that nearly sacred reputation for top-notch golf course designs, as well as, making this project another world-famous links.

In early afternoon, when the presenter finally got around to speaking about the basic price issues, I heard the lower jaws of those assembled hit the table simultaneously which made for a resounding thud! He was talking about a multi-million-dollar proposal. The steering committee members were absolutely shocked! They were in total disbelief. He concluded his presentation, asked if there were any questions. He then thanked the group for their time and noted that he had to drive about 100 miles back to Duluth to catch his plane. He left.

There I sat there in silence with the stunned committee members.

Not really certain of what to do or, if appropriate, what to say, I began to speak to the group about what an honor it had been for me to be in the presence of a representative of this world-renowned golf course designer. I shared how I was overwhelmed, as I'm sure they were, with the presentation, the credentials, the world-wide scope of the organization. I thanked the committee for including me in this meeting. Unable to think of anything further of worth to say, I sat there in silence for what seemed like forever.

After an extended period of silence, one of the committee members finally asked me who I was and what I was doing at their meeting.

After introducing myself, I shared with them that I was a golf course construction contractor and that I had been invited by one of their resort owner members. I went on to say that presently my crew and I were working on a nine-hole addition project in Deerwood, Minnesota. I noted that the project I was currently working was designed by a well-known golf course architect of solid renown in the upper mid-west from Edina, Minnesota. I shared with them that the price for that nine-hole addition was just over half a million dollars. This time the silence seemed to last even longer than before when the "big league" guy finished up with his presentation. I guess they couldn't believe what I had just shared with them concerning price.

Finally, they began to ask me questions – about my experience, references, contacts, methods of construction, and advantages of this and that, etc., etc. I saw I that I had an opportunity to take control of the meeting and I did so.

First of all, I explained to them that my wife and I owned a cabin at Grand Marias, which made us property owners in Cook County - their county. Because of that, I was very familiar with the area. I shared some observations about the area which I didn't know if they had thought a lot about. This new golf course they were thinking of having built was 100 miles from the two nearest communities of any size at all in the region. On the U.S. side of the border, it was Duluth, Minnesota to the southwest. At nearly the same distance, it was Thunder Bay, Ontario, to the northeast on the Canadian side of the border. It was hard to believe that golfers would enjoy flying into either of these cities and then drive an additional two hours on a two-lane road to golf at such a remote golf course – whomever designed it. Although the Minnesota's North Shore of Lake Superior was becoming a more popular tourist destination, it just seemed hard to believe that a multi-million-dollar 18-hole golf course could "make it" financially.

Another factor which should be considered too was local weather conditions which would make for a very short golfing season on Lake Superiors Northern Shore. These two factors, among others, would certainly limit revenues for any area golf course project.

I suggested that they contact the architect from Edina, Minnesota, to design the golf course for them. His fees to do the design would be substantially less than those charged by the world-renowned designer. Besides, this designer was from Minnesota and that alone would give the project more of a local flavor and, certainly, more local interest.

It was late afternoon when I finished up and time for me to leave the meeting and head back to my job in Deerwood. I thanked the committee again for inviting me and wished them all the best with the future of their project. I left not really knowing if I had made a favorable impact on the group at the meeting or not. I did feel that I had shared good information with them and that I had given them some ideas to think about.

The spring of 1988 looked promising. We had the project at Deerwood to finish. I was dealing on a nine-hole expansion project in Red Wing, Minnesota, a nine-hole remodeling project in Duluth, Minnesota, and a nine-hole expansion project in Baraboo, Wisconsin. I was successful in negotiating projects both in Red Wing and Duluth, Minnesota. I was the low bidder on the Baraboo, Wisconsin, project. We had one job from the previous season to finish and three new projects to start in the spring. It was that wonderful madness all over again.

The work season started off in early April when the crew was dispatched back to Deerwood to complete the finishing work on that project. Both of the projects in Red Wing and Duluth were commenced in early May. In order to get both of these new projects moving, some personnel and equipment was removed from Deerwood and sent to these two new jobs.

Suddenly the euphoria of this tremendous amount of work ended and we hadn't even started the Baraboo project as yet. The abundant workload and necessity of having to utilize "thin crews" on all projects made clear the reality of having overstepped our firm's capacity. The most difficult problem to deal with was that of the shortage of experienced personnel. Not only were we really stretched thin, our projects were so geographically spread out. These factors made management of these projects really, really tough. It would be fair to say that, to use business management language, I was "firefighting". I was throwing as many resources as can be mustered to put out the worst fire (meaning biggest problem). In some cases, I threw less than fully experienced people into project management positions and hoped like hell they would figure out a way to get work done in my absence. Crews were shuffled between jobs just to make some sort of job progress happen in an attempt to pacify project owners, designers and architects. I knew I was operating on the edge of disaster and that I had no choice but to push on, move forward and keep trying to make progress on all of these projects as best my personnel and I could.

Starting at 4:00 a.m. was a typical workday for me that summer. Most of those days ended between 10:00 and 11:00 p.m. It really doesn't take all that long for this level of craziness to take its toll on one's physical and mental well-being. Add to that, 45,000 – 50,000 road miles driving between these jobs – all within roughly a seven-month period adds quite a load to one's stress level. The miles alone wouldn't have been so bad except that while traveling between these jobs to "put out the fires", the brain is being fried figuring, sorting out details, planning and worrying. It's a completely relentless mental strain.

Due to exceeding our capacity to perform the work under contract and the other factors mentioned above, there were an unusually large number of problems to be dealt with at all times. It seemed as though everything was going against the planning I was doing. Though I knew I was operating on overload, I refused to quit because I knew quitting was not an option. I had to push ahead no matter what. The only way out of the predicament I had placed my firm and myself in was to fight it out. As I dealt with the problems and kept coming up with solutions, the next problem would arise.

As the season progressed, the pressure eased temporarily in early June when the Deerwood project was completed. This freed up much needed experienced personnel to be moved to either Duluth or Red Wing. However, this was about the same time as the Baraboo project needed to be started.

There were certain unique factors on all three projects just to ensure that my stress level was kept dangerously high. My newly appointed project superintendent for the Baraboo project had some limited golf course construction knowledge and experience. As an example of the problems I faced, my new man on the job worked with a subcontractor to whom I had "subbed" the earthmoving portion of the work. Naturally, my "sub" was to work under the direction of my firm's project superintendent. This very experienced earthmoving contractor, I think, could "smell blood". I believe that he could tell that my man didn't really have the experience necessary to manage the project. Because of this, the earthmoving contractor, working at hourly rates for his machinery with operators furnished, could have been far more efficient had he been given proper direction and had his work been better managed for him. Being stretched way too thin myself, I could really not fault my limited-experience project superintendent nor my subcontractor for the inefficiencies of the earthmoving on the project. No. It was my fault that I wasn't there to help my man keep these costs in line. This inefficiency cost the firm a lot of time and money.

The Duluth job was a real dandy. *I was lied to.* Unbeknown to me, the golf course I was working on hadn't secured their financing prior to awarding the contract to my firm. We were working on the project, paying wages, purchasing fuel, paying for insurance and all the other business expenses without my client having made arrangements for paying me. No revenue from a project will give a business owner a little something extra to think about while traveling between jobs. Since they were not paying me in accordance with the terms and conditions of the contract, I pulled crew members off that job and sent them to the other two projects. I maintained only a "skeleton crew" there until they started to pay me. I was going to keep up my end of the contract, though on small scale, even if they were not keeping theirs.

Thank GOD for the Red Wing project. It went the best of all three projects. This project covered the costs for the other two until the financing and the resulting payments to my firm got worked out on Duluth project.

The projects were completed by late November except for the Baraboo job. The irrigation installation contractor, who was working under separate contract for the golf course at Baraboo, had never done golf course work before. It was his inexperience and the resulting delays caused by this lack of experience which prevented our firm from finishing the job that season.

During late November 1988, an opportunity to bid a project in western Wisconsin at Amery came up. I bid the project and won. This project was to be worked through the winter months. This was my first time trying to do work in the frozen earth in the winter months in Wisconsin. We moved on the job right after the holiday season in early January 1989. It was a mild winter up to that point and everything on the job seemed to be going along quite well. Our progress was beyond my expectations. We made such a good showing initially that club members started talking about an early completion of the job. But good old Wisconsin winter reminded us in short order who was really in control of the project. Winter suddenly got real nasty. Temperatures would eventually plummet to -30 F with wind chills at -55 F. Welcome to Wisconsin winter.

One day when it was around -15 F, we arrived at the jobsite at 7:00 a.m. and tried to start the cold equipment. One bulldozer out of the four started while the other three wouldn't even cough. We used jumper cables, ether, built charcoal fires under the oil pans – everything to try to get those cold machines started. The machines made up their minds that they were not going to run. After working all morning, we finally had all four machines running around noon. Half of a work day wasted. That day I made several decisions about temperature conditions related to winter work in general. If the temperature was not at least 0 F or above, we would not go to the job and we would not attempt to start cold equipment. Weather permitting, we worked through the winter months on the Amery job.

Progress slowed as the ground thawed that spring and we were now facing spring mud. The muddy conditions caused a drop in our productivity. This drop in productivity as well as other factors caused our working relationship with the club's representative to deteriorate. What had previously been rather congenial discussions in the recent past were now becoming shouting matches. There were accusations and threats flying all over the place. This deteriorated working relationship became personal.

I needed to receive funds from the project to pay business expenses but the club refused to pay based on a technicality in the contract. The project architect had suffered a major heart attack and was hospitalized for an extended period of time after quadruple bypass surgery. Besides his time in the hospital, naturally, he needed additional recovery time at home. Therefore, he was unable to make monthly inspection tours of the project to determine the percentage of the work completed and to "sign off" on the pay request of the contractor - me. The actual contract wording said, "The golf course architect shall make periodic tours of the construction project to determine the percentage of completion of the work and based solely on this estimate the contractor shall be paid."

The club's main representative for the project was a local banker who was an arrogant jerk (it would be easy to use "CONSTRUCTIONESE" when referring to this guy, but I'll spare you that). I guess he had a real need to look the part of a "big shot" in his small community. He chose to read the contract in its most literal interpretation when I requested a "draw".

He asked me, in front of a number of other club members, **"What's the matter with you, BOY? Are you illiterate? Read the contract. It says that the architect shall determine the percentage of comple-**

tion, and it looks like he can't make that determination given his health condition."

Smirking at me entirely in his best interest of putting on a grandiose public display of his position of power, he explained in front of the gathered group, that if the architect was indeed unable to review the project to ascertain a percentage of completion, well, that's just too bad.

"No money for you, BOY!", he said, in front of the gathering inside the clubhouse. What a world class jerk! I'll admit I got wild when this showoff publicly humiliated me, as was his goal and which he so thoroughly accomplished.

This is what this job degenerated to. I was stretched to the breaking point financially. I was emotionally drained given this foolish war-like atmosphere I was subjected to on a daily basis by. After much negotiation and a lot of wasted time, I was at length, being reduced to that of a mere beggar with this haughty, self-righteous banker. All of this, I believe, was done entirely for his personal enjoyment and satisfaction. He wasn't even attempting to be right with me about the progress of the project.

I finally did get paid after an associate of the architect was sent to the job to determine the percentage of completion. This was after the banker jerk had the gall to disturb the recovering architect at his home about this payment issue. Working in the adversarial environment unnecessarily created on this jobsite, and constantly struggling to keep my company's cash flow flowing, I needed another project.

That spring of 1989, an opportunity came to my attention and I jumped at it.

I was contacted to take a look at a nine-hole addition to the golf course in New Glarus, Wisconsin. That project was in Green County – the Swiss settlement – the land of my forefathers. I certainly had to take a look at this job.

This was a unique job. The Edelweiss Chalet Golf Course had hired a designer to do a routing plan for the addition but had not, as yet, worked out the detailed drawings for the greens or tees or traps. I offered that I could save them a pile of money because I could "field design" these golf course features for them on a hole-by-hole basis. By that time in my career, I had built a plenty of tees, greens and sand traps and said I knew how to make these features fit the land. If they would be willing to leave the design of these details of the project up to me, I could build these features. But that all of this work would have to be approved and accepted by the club's representative. They agreed.

This was my first shot at design/build and I loved it. I sold them on the advantages of a design/build project. I offered a price to do the work and sold the job to these Swiss people of my family's heritage.

The folks at new Glarus had paid me a sizable down payment on their project at the time we signed the contract. Because of receiving this down-payment when I needed it so badly for my financially hurting company, I felt dutybound to run this project personally. I left an experienced project superintendent in charge of the finishing work (at that time it was really all we had left to do) on the Amery, Wisconsin, project. With a tiny crew, I headed off to New Glarus to work on that golf course.

At New Glarus, my crew members and I were treated with kindness, respect, appreciation and general good will. We were made to feel at home, to feel welcome in the community. This was a totally different work environment from the battlefield atmosphere in Amery, Wisconsin. It was easy to see a marked improvement in the crew's attitude and work habits as a result of this environment as opposed to the treatment we had been subjected to for the last several months at on the Amery job. The New Glarus job flowed so smoothly that we completed the nine-hole addition – start-to-finish – in 69 consecutive working days. Along with the smoothness of the job flow, the money flowed into the company to make up for the unfortunate situation on the job in Amery, Wisconsin.

The lessons learned over the last five or so years had been tough to take. I know I grew as a businessman and I also know that the net worth of the company grew fourfold. Many risks had been taken, but the company's growth made all of these risks and the headaches and the heartaches seem worthwhile. All in all, we had done quite well since my father's death. In business terms, we had been successful.

MY DREAM JOB

Spring of 1989 had been quite a hectic mess to say the least. The western Wisconsin job had not been good due to cash flow problems. The cash flow problems were based on differences of opinion which brought about the resulting personality clashes. I felt I should be paid and the banker, again wanting to "throw his weight around", didn't think so. The job in New Glarus covered the unwarranted and tragic financial mess in Amery, Wisconsin. We had had two jobs going at once – one to finish up and a new one to start. Then another opportunity came along that I absolutely couldn't pass up. This was an opportunity to have my dream job!

The Edina, Minnesota, based golf course architect had been hired to design the golf course project at Lutsen, Minnesota, as I had recommended to the committee two years previously. The jobsite was 17 miles from my wife's and my newly completed log cabin on the shore of Lake Superior. I knew the people involved in the project and was very familiar with the jobsite, the soil conditions, area contractors and suppliers. I was sent a set of plans and the bidding documents. The bid date for the project was to be June 25th, 1989 – one day before my 39th birthday.

I spent a lot of time in the area meeting with the contractors and suppliers to talk over pricing for the supplies and materials required for the project. I studied the job from all the possible angles I could imagine to attempt to work these angles to my advantage. This was my dream job and I was going to do whatever it took to see to it that I won the bid.

Study and figure, figure and study. Think and re-think. Try the numbers again. I figured the bid 5 different ways. Then I picked what I thought were the most realistic components of each of the 5 bid methods I had figured. Combining these numbers, I arrived at my price to build this championship level eighteen-hole golf course. I was completely frazzled. I anguished over the all the possibilities, all of the combinations and all of the details surrounding the job.

The scheduled bid opening was at 3:00 p.m. on Friday, June 25th, 1989. I filled in the numbers on the bid sheet, sealed it along with my bid bond in the envelope and delivered it that day to the Cook County Court House in downtown Grand Marais, Minnesota, per instructions just after lunch. Upon my return from delivering the bid, I made reservations for my wife and I at our favorite area restaurant for that evening.

My wife and I spent an hour or so milling around town before we went to the bid opening. As is my habit, we were there at the courthouse for the bid opening way before we needed to be, just waiting. I was nervous.

The bidding process was quite different in Cook County, Minnesota, from elsewhere where I have submitted bids. Usually, the bid opening process is quite a formal ordeal. Professionals wearing suits and ties, open bids and read the contents in a rather formal, regimented procedure. Not so here, evidently.

Four sealed bid envelopes were brought into the courtroom and placed on one of the lawyer's tables near the front of the room by a nicely dressed young lady from the county clerk's office. The bids included submissions from two Minnesota based contractors, one from the state of Virginia and mine. The only two bidders present were a Minnesota competitor and myself. I was a wreck! My wife tried to get me to settle down but it was useless.

I was making small talk with this representative of one of the Minnesota based competitors whom I'd come to know over the years from other bid openings in the past. He was talking about a job we had both bid which he had won on another golf course in Duluth. We talked about other jobs we had competed with one another on over the years. In truth, both of us were desperately trying to put the upcoming moment of truth out of our thoughts and we both knew that.

So far – so good. But there ended the similarities with all previous bid openings I had ever attended.

Other concerned parties were pacing around in the courthouse central hallway. Several of the golf course steering committee members whom I had met with two years ago were present out of curiosity. I suppose they wanted to find out who the contractor would be to build the golf course.

Somewhere around 3:00 p.m. a guy raised his voice to be heard above the conversations going on to tell all concerned parties to please have a seat in the courtroom where the bids were going to be opened. All those present from the hall funneled into the courtroom and had a seat. Then, the fun began.

First, this guy who invited everyone into the courtroom quietly moves to the front of the room and just stands there more of less gazing at the assembled group. There he stood. As he was gazing at the people in the room, I was scoping this guy out. Receding hairline with thinning gray hair – very scraggly and unkept. Wire rimmed glasses with frames that had obviously been more-or-less fixed in a haphazard manner too many times. Scruffy, unkept beard on a very narrow thin face. His plain gray sweatshirt had been washed so many times that there were holes developing all over it and the sleeves were cut off and frayed – the left one below the elbow in length and the right one slightly above the elbow. He must have loved that tattered sweatshirt for some reason or he'd have thrown it away. The elasticity of the neckband and the waistband had been "shot" for some time. His pants were work style dungarees complete with hammer loop and plier pocket. These too had been washed so many times that they were giving way in the knees. There were thin spots on the thighs as well as certain areas of the long worn-out seams. No socks, just crummy looking, dirty, cheap, worn-out boat-deck style sneakers completed the ensemble.

"Hey", he asked, "has anybody here ever been to one of these deals before? I mean, like, I've really never have done one of these deals before now and they asked me to do it, and you know, like, I really don't know how to go about this - really! Oh, by the way, I should introduce myself. I'm the committee's legal-council."

WOW! So much for the professionals in suits and ties!

I said nothing right away but I couldn't help thinking to myself – what the hell is going on here anyway? I looked at my competitor and he looked at me in total disbelief. Together, more or less taking turns, we explained how the process was to be handled for this lawyer's benefit.

He asked, "OK, who are you two guys? I want to know because I'll read your bids first since you were interested enough in the project to come all the way up here to listen to this stuff." We introduced ourselves and he pulled our envelopes.

He opened my competitors bid first, reading it aloud just as we had instructed. He also acknowledged the attached bid bond in amount of 10% of the bid price, again, as we instructed him to do. My competitors bid was better than $100,000.00 above my price. I had beaten him but now, how about the other two. He opened and read my bid next and announced the price and the attached bid bond. This bid of mine was the largest amount I had ever written on a bid form - $1,111,777.00. The other two bids were higher than mine also. In construction contracting language, I was the "apparent low bidder" on my dream job! I had WON!

Since the committee members present knew me from the meeting nearly two years before, they all rushed over to shake my hand and offer their congratulations. They all said they had hoped I'd win the bid. I told them I had hoped they'd write me an exclusive contract based on a negotiated price rather than having to go through the stress of this bidding process. They laughed. They asked if my wife and I would like to go somewhere to have a drink to celebrate the victory. I invited them all to follow my wife and I back to our cabin which they did. We drank and talked about the great golf course to be built by my firm. It was a great feeling to know that this job was mine after all the time I'd spent preparing for this project. The job was mine and that was all that really mattered to me now.

The committee members left our cabin and we drove back into town for our dinner at our favorite restaurant. Upon arrival, we were greeted by the owners. We were seated at the best table in the house and congratulated on submitting the winning bid on the golf course construction project. There at the table was a bucket with a bottle of champagne, compliments of the restauranteur. Oh my, how fast news travels in a small community! The bid opening had taken place less than two hours before our arrival at the restaurant and already the apparent low bidder was public knowledge. There are no secrets in a small town. What a wonderful day-before-my-birthday day it was! My wife called me her million-dollar man. It was a great feeling that evening to have won my dream job on the eve of my 39th birthday.

The following Monday it was time to face reality again. There were still two jobs to be completed. Despite the recurring day-to-day problems associated with these construction projects, everything seemed to go much better now that I had this big job to look forward to this fall.

As that summer of 1989 wore on, the projects that were underway approached completion. As previously mentioned, the New Glarus job went extremely well. Never before had we completed a nine-hole project in such a short period of time. As previously mentioned, the Amery job went extremely poorly. Never before had I had to deal in such an adversarial environment. I was looking beyond my immediate circumstances towards the day when we could begin to move equipment to the Lutsen job.

Around mid-summer, I got a call from the Lutsen committee chairman asking if I knew of any golf course superintendents who would be interested in the job at the as yet unbuilt project. The committee decided that they wanted to hire a person for this position even before construction began. That way their golf course superintendent would know everything about the project and the golf course itself "from the get-go" – "from the ground up". Did I know of anyone? I told them that I had just the right guy for them and he was working just 100 miles down the north shore in Duluth

I had gained a whole lot of respect for the golf course superintendent at the project we had built in Duluth two years back. He really knew how to take care of a golf course and it was obvious that he was one of the top three people in this position whom I'd ever met. He was one of those rare greenskeepers who could "read" the turf. That is to say, he was one of those guys who could look at turf grass and know what the grass needed to make the golf course look as near perfect as possible.

I came to appreciate his know-how and his management of his crew when I saw how he kept this golf course in Duluth. He was getting the job done despite the fact that he was doing the job working with junk equipment, no budget and a crew comprised of minimum-wage youngsters. He was amazing! And then, he told me of how these cheapskates on the club's board of directors, who had lied to me about project finances, could do nothing but bitch and complain about the condition of the golf course. Nothing he did was right according to them. It was out of pure respect for his abilities that I wanted him to get away from these arrogant wannabees. His was only his name that I offered up to the committee. They hired him.

Just a side note; I guess I developed a rather strange way to evaluate the skill of a golf course superintendent over my years of golf course construction. It was this. How did the edges of the sand traps appear? Were these edges cut sharp and crisp or were the edges shaggy and unkept? I looked at it this way; If the superintendent had managed his crew so effectively that he had all of the turf on the golf course looking perfect and yet had time for the crew to keep those sand trap edges cut clean and sharp, well now, there was a terrific superintendent.

The Lutsen contract was signed and delivered in the first week of September. The bond and all of the contract documents were in order and we were given the "go ahead". We began to move equipment to the job on September 13th. I will never ever begin a project on the 13th of any month.

My tractor/trailer rig hauling the first load of equipment to the project "dropped a valve" in the diesel engine causing major engine failure which required a complete engine overhaul. Without an operational engine in my main haul truck, I utilized another old track/tractor in the fleet and hired some of the trucking done by another firm. Two weeks and $7,000.00 later, my truck was back on the road. What a great way to begin a project.

We did get the equipment moved to the job and began the clearing phase of the project (removal of trees and stumps – land clearing is a commonly used term for this phase of a construction project). 120 acres of tree and stumps were cut out of the thick, pristine forest to make room for fairways, tees, greens and traps. During this phase of the project there were 9 bulldozers of various sizes at work spread out over approximately 600 acres. The clearing boundaries had been marked out prior to the start of this portion of the work by the newly hired golf course superintendent.

Other than a few breakdowns, the job was moving along quite well. As winter began to show signs of early arrival, we were nearly finished with the clearing phase of the job. We were actually beginning to rough shape some of the greens and tee mounding on some of the holes. Winter winds, snowfall and freezing soil conditions closed the project down for the season on November 15th. We left the equipment parked in neat rows and retreated to Eau Claire for the winter months.

The 1989-90 winter passed but seemed to drag on forever. The commercial snow removal business (the firm's winter income producer) was really slow since there was minimal snowfall during the entire winter season. Repair work on equipment was rather limited since much of the equipment fleet was left on the Lutsen jobsite. My anxiety to get back to work on the golf course project made the days seem to pass even slower than would have needed to be. I was so wanting get back to work on that golf course.

Towards mid-March, I began to make calls on a daily basis to the golf course superintendent inquiring about weather conditions and moisture conditions at the jobsite. March dragged on into early April with no real break in the weather conditions on Lake Superior's North Shore. I drove up to look over the situation and decided to have some crew members report to the job on April 10th to begin to check-over and service all of the machines so that we could begin the construction again this spring. One week later, the entire crew was back on the job and the golf course was again under construction.

During the summer months, we experienced the usual amount of bad weather, breakdowns and other normal run of problems to be faced in earthwork construction. All things considered, however, the job progressed quite well. The greens, tees and sand traps all took shape despite the washouts and mud caused by the rainstorms. Fairway contours and rolls continued to improve as the days passed. The crew worked well together and had a genuine *espirit de corps*. I was really enjoying working with this group of dedicated individuals. We left the project for the Memorial Day weekend. It had rained and it was too wet to work anyway.

My birthday came on June 26th (my 40th) and we had a big birthday party/beer party/cookout for the entire crew arranged and catered by my wife. Several of the committee members were in attendance as well as the golf course designer and his wife. This was simply a great end to a great day.

The 4th of July came and went. The crew went home for a break over the national holiday. I continued to work on some detail items on the jobsite. The project was coming together nicely.

We worked through the balance of July and into August, making great progress. As the Labor Day holiday weekend approached, I could clearly see the end of the project. We had commenced the seeding process on certain finished fairways and roughs around mid-July, and this too was progressing very well. We did have several severe rain storms which resulted in repairs to be made, but we were able to overcome these problems. As the end of August approached, I was confident that 10 days, or at the outside, two weeks, would wrap up this project completely.

The entire crew left to spend a few days with their families over the Labor Day holiday weekend. After spending the entire summer living together at our cabin, my wife and I spent our last weekend together there. She would leave for her school teaching job when the weekend was over.

Everything looked promising for a rather quick completion of the job during the next week or so after the holiday. My construction budget was in OK shape. I had funding enough, not abundant, but plenty to complete the project and show a marginal profit besides. Though we had experienced some bad weather, we had overcome it. The weather had taken a toll on my budget, yet under the conditions, I felt the job would turn out to be a winner if only modestly so.

After the Labor Day Holiday weekend, two occurrences took place with regard to the job. The crew returned. So did the rains for the next seven weeks. We could work on the project only during certain "windows of opportunity" afforded us by miserable weather conditions.

Finishing a golf course construction project requires dry weather. In order to establish proper seedbeds so that the seed can actually be incorporated into the soil at the optimal depth, dry – bone dry – soil conditions are necessary. Wet conditions at this stage of a project can be disastrous.

It seemed that whatever we accomplished one day was washed away the following day. This would not have been so bad in and of itself, except for the rocky soil conditions encountered on the Lutsen project. Every repair of rain damage took three to four times as long as it should have to restore a damaged area to pre-rainstorm conditions. Repair work required not only the normally expected re-grading of washouts and rivulets, but it also required very labor-intensive removal of all of the newly exposed rocks and debris which had been brought to the surface as a result of the re-grading. The problem with all this repair work - re-grading, rock picking, soil preparation and re-seeding- is that it adds to the cost of the completed project. The bid price is figured based on doing all of the elemental parts of the job once and only once.

As a contractor competing for a contract in the competitive bidding process, all elements of the project are figured with little contingency for errors or problems. Certainly, there has to be some contingency for weather and other potential problems. However, if a bidder should dwell on too much negativity, a bidder with such an outlook may as well stay home and not bid the project. Normally, a contractor figures the job based on optimal conditions to arrive at a low bid number. This is normal practice. After the optimal condition price has been arrived at, it is only then that contingencies for tough conditions on the job are added on to your low bid to arrive at the final bid price. Add too much and your competitor will have the job and you will be watching rather than doing the job.

At Lutsen, after the Labor Day Holiday weekend, with all the rain and the repair costs going on, there was nothing left but to fight our way to job completion. Most of the fairways and putting surfaces were seeded 6 or 7 times in order to finish the job. The contract bid price remained constant for the project while the costs to finish the contract continued to escalate.

Seven weeks after the Labor Day holiday weekend and some $170,000.00 in losses later, the golf course construction project at Lutsen, Minnesota, was completed. Not only was the job finished, I was finished as a contractor as well. The firm had lost all of its working capital. In other words, the firm was BROKE!

My dream job had cost me my company.

PART IV - BROKE!

HARSH REALITIES

The final inspection of the Lutsen project was completed on October, 16th. 1990. In retrospect, this was fortunate because on the following day, snow began to fall in northern Minnesota. Had we not finished the job when we did, things would have only become worse. We would have had to face returning to the jobsite the following spring to complete the project. That scenario would have been impossible given the crippled financial condition of the business at the time of the project's final inspection.

All of the paperwork was closed out, all of the subcontractors were paid in full, all of the wages were paid to our employees. All of the documents were completed to allow me to pick up my final payment for the completed project. With check in hand, I drove back to our office where I knew we had a number of financial obligations to take care of with short term creditors.

The severe losses at the end of the project depleted our cash reserves and working capital. We had to borrow money on our revolving line of credit for working capital at the bank "maxing it out". Our long-term note was also at its limit. Our firm was $350,000.00 in debt with no money, no work on the horizon, no income to speak of and no real possibilities of securing any work or any other potential income opportunities. This was bleak! Worse yet, I had no idea of what to do or how to proceed.

We moved all of the equipment back to Eau Claire. We had to get the equipment back to our place of business just in case any work came to us in our local area. This only cost us more money of which we had none to spare. We wanted – no needed – to be ready to respond to any opportunities that might come our way. Another reason to move the equipment back is that many of the machines used for the golf course construction business were also used by our firm for the snow removal business.

As soon as I returned from the Lutsen job, I contacted every area business we had ever worked for or with to see if there was any possibility of putting some of our equipment to work to generate some kind of income for the firm no matter how much or how little. There was nothing. I would have done nearly anything to save the company from what I knew was coming. I prayed for the worst winter on record with the most snowfall ever for our region. I was hoping snow removal could save us. That 1990-91 winter season, it hardly snowed at all compared to previous winters. I was stuck in a terrible situation.

I searched trade journals for opportunities. All of the publicly bid projects required bonding. I knew that I didn't have a prayer of securing a bond given the recent financial tumble our firm had just taken. I found myself in a position I had never before experienced in my business career or my personal life. I was BROKE! As a result, I was in a position, an entrapped predicament impoverished people all over the world find themselves suffering through. I was completely powerless and my choices were severely limited.

The firm had suffered a severe financial failure and we were continuing in a downward spiral. The importance of financial liquidity became absolutely clear to me at this desperate time because I no longer had financial liquidity. While certain assets are necessary to the operations of any business, liquidity of capital is far more vital. I found this out in a hurry when I tried to continue to operate a business with no working capital and no chance of obtaining any. Assets are not cash. It takes a long time turn assets into cash to pay down debt. The time factor to turn assets into cash was working against me because the interest clock on the loans keeps on ticking away. This further depleted my asset's base value. The interest on the debt load was literally eating up my company's assets. How does one go about applying the brakes?

Richard L. Freitag

I had no idea things could get this bad!

FACING OTHERS

What a heavy responsibility it is to have employees. Employees and their family's wellbeing are your responsibility as a businessperson and yours alone. I convened a meeting to tell them that I had failed. I further told them that I would help every last one of them to secure good jobs with other area contractors in the upcoming season. I kept my word on assisting them to find employment for all who wished to be assisted in this process.

Having to explain to my employees that I had failed them was one of the toughest jobs I have ever had. Then watching as your trained, skilled, knowledgeable, dedicated and devoted employees take leave of you and your failed company is a gut-wrenching experience. MY GOD! How I hated to see them go. Yet I knew I had no choice if I wanted to be honest and right with them and myself. I did all that I could do to be right with my employees.

Maybe it's just this town, but I don't believe the "word on the street" of my business failure could have been made public knowledge any faster if I'd have done a press release or news segment on the local TV station. Local business people whom I had known for years knew I had taken a terrible beating on my last project. As a result, they distanced themselves from me. Although I had been a long-time member of several area business organizations and other groups, suddenly, things were different now. I was an outcast. The cordial business conversations of the past were not so cordial anymore. Instead of the old "How are things going for you and your business these days?" or

"How's business?", the questions became totally different. Conversations sunk low to things like, "Is it true that you're lost your shorts on that job up north?" or my favorite, "What are you going to do now that you're broke?"

Now I've been in awkward, uncomfortable situations before in my life, but to have to look another business person in the eye and admit that you have failed on a grand scale takes awkward and uncomfortable to entirely new lows. It is strange how people, and especially business people, will distance themselves from a loser. Being broke, I found that I always had plenty of room around me. Actually, I had a disquieting amount of room around me given the distancing by former associates.

Employees and associates were easy to deal with compared to creditors. But dealing with others gets even better yet. There are the bankers to face which is another story entirely.

My sister and I decided to go on offence. We composed a letter and sent a copy to all of our creditors. We explained our financial situation to them and assured them that we would pay all of our outstanding bills along with all the accrued interest on the balances due them. We promised that even if we were forced to liquidate all of our business assets, we would pay off everyone completely. Among other things, we explained that we had suffered a serious financial setback on the project in northern Minnesota during the past business season and that the limited snowfall of the winter months caused further difficulties. As a result of this nonexistent cash flow and our tough financial position, we would be unable to pay for the next several months. We said that by May we would be able to pay again when we began to generate a cash flow. We asked our creditors for their patience. The letter concluded by stating once again that we certainly had adequate assets to cover any and all of our obligations and that we would, if necessary, liquidate our entire company to meet our obligations to them.

Without exception, every last one of our creditors agreed to go along with us through the winter months. Some even sent letters thanking us for our business in the past and the recent letter clarifying our situation. Many asked what they could do to help us including, unbelievably, extending us more credit to get us through the winter months. It had paid to go on offence. Amazing!

Our fiscal year ended September 30th. We had our financial statements back from our CPAs in early January of 1991. The income statement showed a loss of $170,000.00 for the past year's operations. We knew we had to face the bankers with this devastating document showing this terrible loss. But the how does one look that banker in the eye with such a disastrous year end statements and then tell him at the time that in short order you will be unable to make your monthly payments on your bank loans?

Again, my sister and I went on offence. Before our meeting with the banker to go over our year end financials, we decided that we were going to be as prepared as possible. We planned to answer his all of questions and have a "comeback" response for his comments on the past year's terrible performance. We wanted "our ducks in a row". We typed up lists explaining the loss on the Lutsen job listing over a dozen factors which had adversely affected the project – mostly weather conditions along with the dates of the most severe problems and the resultant loss due to these factors. Additionally, we formulated a list of our assets with "fire sale" prices if we were to liquidate them at an auction sale based on published auction results from around the nation. I believe that the most important decision we made was to have the meeting held at our place of business rather than the banker's office. This put him on "our turf" which I still believe had a most positive impact on the outcome of the meeting.

We had switched banks to our present one a number of years prior to our 1990 loss. The bank we had been with previously didn't really wish to do business anymore with contractors. It was an easy choice to make when deciding which bank to go with after the last one. For years I had been a member of an area volunteer service club, The Sunrise Exchange Club (Like other service clubs such as; Lions, Kiwanis, Optimists, etc.) and had known a banker member of the club for some time. We'll just call him "Pete" for this portion of the story and I was certainly thankful to have him as our banker.

Pete arrived at our office late that morning. After some small talk he had a seat and we presented him with our financial statements. Before he opened the folder, we informed him that we had suffered a terrible financial loss from operations this previous season. Pete opened the folder and studied the contents. After a few moments, and with a completely expressionless face, he looked up at both of us and said, "You said it was going to be bad but I had no idea you meant this bad!" He went on to say, "Even if you had anything left on your line of credit, under these conditions, it's all over."

We handed Pete our lists, one at a time. He studied each one carefully. I believe that he thought our preparation efforts were a statement by us of our intentions to meet our obligations. I believe too that he knew us well enough to know that we were steadfast in our commitment to do everything we could to liquidate our debt without declaring bankruptcy.

I spoke. I said, "Pete, we know we are in tough shape. We also understand that you and the bank have all of business assets tied up in the "General Business Security Agreement" (our loan). Under these conditions, naturally, it will be your call as to how we are to proceed under these conditions. Within one month we will no longer be able to make our monthly payment on the loan to the bank and further realize that we will be in default at that time. It is our intention, with your permission, to sell off the assets of the firm and to use the proceeds from those sales to pay down our debt load as quickly as we are able. During the winter months, construction equipment and trucks do not sell very well in the upper mid-west. With your permission, we will advertise the list of saleable assets in nationally circulated trade publications to try to make something positive happen for our firm. We guarantee that the bank will be made whole through these efforts. We fully realize and acknowledge that the bank, being the note holder, has the option of holding an auction sale to liquidate our business to satisfy the bank notes. An auction is a free-for-all with usually poor, rock-bottom prices on vehicles and equipment and I personally believe that such a sale would seriously hurt the bank as well as our firm."

"If you would let me handle the selloff these assets," I continued, "I will be able to get good prices for this equipment. I know the history of each piece and I know the local contractors who would be interested in purchasing these things. I can sell these items at higher than auction prices to area contractors who know that we have an excellent maintenance program and keep our fleet in tip-top condition. This is a win-win option for the bank's good as well as ours. I realize that the choice is yours to make, but the auction route is clearly a very risky venture. It's up to you."

Pete's response really caught me off guard. He said, "First of all, at least at this time, your payments to the bank are current. Presently, your only problem is that you have horrific financial statements. In truth, you will not be in real trouble with the bank until six months after you fail to make your monthly payments. At that time, the bank will step in if you are still unable to meet your obligations. Naturally, I will have to share the bad news in your financials with my board of directors. In the meantime, do whatever you can to make the next payment. If that's not possible, it's not possible. As far as liquidation of your assets is concerned, we don't want to have an auction any more than you do. We look at auctions as a last resort where everybody except the auctioneer loses. I'll talk over your proposal to sell down your own assets with the board and get back to you in a day or two. For now, think of any avenues of opportunity to look into to try to help your present situation."

With that said, Pete left our office.

I was a nervous wreck. Now our financial statements would be reviewed by the board of directors who were led by the president of the bank. The newly appointed bank president, I was told, would sell out his own mother to recoup bank losses. A world class heartless bastard among heartless bastards!

Pete was a bank vice-president. I believe, and I always will, that if we'd have had a lesser man than Pete looking out for our best interests and had Pete not had the faith in me that he did, we would have been sold out under the most unfavorable terms. I will believe this until the day I die. We were fortunate to have a banker with heart. A man who could look at certain "intangibles" and look beyond the obvious disaster to see the potential in the company and the people involved in its operations. Thank GOD there are still some bankers, some individuals of solid character who still trust people worthy of trust and still believe that there are people of whom it is said, "He is a man of his word."

Pete had intervened on our behalf with the bank president and the board of directors and prevailed. True to his word, he did call back in two days. He said, "What you said made good sense. We'll give you six months to see how you do selling-off your vehicles and equipment."

How weird it was. I was now in charge of handling my own demise.

I now had six months in which to demonstrate my good faith to the bank.

SHATTERED SELF

I was broke. The meeting with Pete showed it if I had any doubts about it whatsoever. I was really no longer in control of my business situation other than being the chief salesman relegated to liquidate the company's assets. Other than selling off company assets, now others, not me, were telling me what I could and could not do in my business. I hated being basically dismissed to such a position of servitude. I had always "called my own shots". This was no longer the case given my present business/financial position.

I began to look back on my dream job. How could that job have gone so wrong for me? What could I have done differently so that I could have avoided this calamity I was presently being forced to live through? Why had all of this misfortune happened to me? I was feeling so depressed and all of these questions were repeated day after day after day. I kept on with the "what if's".

As a result of my continuing to question myself about my failure as a businessman, I began to question my human failings to the point of completely losing any and all faith in myself. My self-confidence left town. I was so depressed that, at one point, I even questioned whether it was worth living. Given the miserable failure I viewed myself to have become dwelling in this cesspool of self-pity and negativism, I was wallowing - drowning in this self-imposed mental state of feeling sorry for myself. I had fallen into a trap that others who have experienced my miserable situation have mistakenly taken as fact. Equating the worth of my person to the worth of the things and stuff I had gathered around me is the essence of materialism. Although I didn't understand it at the time, our self-worth as a human being has nothing whatsoever to do with things and stuff.

When not feeling sorry for myself, my time was spent trying to figure out how to overcome being broke. When your best prospects to get out of your financial dilemma are The Publishers Clearing House Sweepstakes or hitting the jackpot in the Lotto Game, I can tell you that you have a problem. I know because I have been there. The problems are so many and so overwhelming. Answers are few. You fry what's left of your mind looking for elusive solutions which make even the slightest amount of sense. When feeling sorry for oneself, solutions do not come – cannot come at all.

Thank GOD, I've never been a drinker nor a doper. I suppose if I had been, I'd have tried to find my way out of my problems in a bottle, a pill, a needle or endlessly smoking joints to maintain a constant high. I did none of these things. At best, I believe, these are temporary escapes from reality or crutches to lean on and certainly no solution to problems of any sort. These temporary fixes only cause further problems over time.

Thank GOD too, for genuine, true friends who stuck by me when I was down. They would listen to me as I shared my situation with them. While there was really nothing they could do for me other than being a "sounding board", they were there for me when I needed them most. Their listening, their empathizing helped me a great deal. That precious time spent with those few true friends I still had left, afforded me a break from my self-destructive tendencies. When alone again, it was back to that same pattern of self-doubt, self-pity and negativism.

For months on end, the dark pattern repeated itself on a daily basis. As a result of this negativity, I lost hair, lost sleep, and lost composure as I wallowed in this mire of self-pity. The worry, the grief and the burned-out mind were all symptoms of the prolonged dwelling of this self-created atmosphere of self-destruction. This time in my life can best be summed up as a complete and total waste of time. This self-inflicted feeling sorry for myself time-wasting went on for close to two years.

PART V – A BREAK FROM BROKE

INTERMISSION MISSION

I have served as a Scoutmaster of a Boy Scout Troop for some time. I continue to be involved with the scouting program because I am the benefactor of having been a Scout in my youth. Daily, I still feel and see the marvelous and positive impact of my scout training as a youth although this training happened decades ago. I feel a deep sense of gratitude to the great men who shared their time and knowledge with me in my youth through the scouting program. I can never repay those men for all they shared with me back then but I can try to share this gift with youngsters today. I have done so for many years and I continue to do so. Currently, I'm a 60-year veteran of the organization.

The scouts in my troop never knew of the financial difficulties I was experiencing at the time of my business failure. It was nothing they needed to know. Furthermore, it would have been wrong of me to allow them to even think that something might happen to the continuity of our troop's program just because I was having trouble in business. My financial problems had nothing to do with the troop's operations.

Every Monday night I would put on a happy face to attend the troop meeting. These meetings were my escape from the nearly constant agonizing at this miserable time in my life. Sharing my scoutcraft knowledge with the scouts in my troop every week was welcome relief from the doldrums of a dormant, nearly dead business.

Each year, before our yearly scouting program takes off, we set up a schedule of events, a calendar for the year which allowed both membership and leadership to know what's going on from week to week. Troop 30, my troop, schedules three Courts of Honor (award ceremonies where Scouts are recognized for their rank advancement as well as other accomplishments) each year – fall, mid-winter and spring After a year of agonizing over my business situation, I was looking forward to the February 10th, 1992, event. I would throw myself into the preparations for this award ceremony. This would be my escape from the torment for a brief time and I needed the escape at that time.

As February 1992 approached, Troop 30 had nine scouts who had joined the troop at the same time who were getting close to completing their work on their Eagle Scout Award (the highest rank awarded by the Boy Scouts of America)., I knew we were going to have Eagle Scouts at the February Court of Honor.

In my youth, I had been awarded the rank of Eagle Scout. I had been one of seven recipients of that coveted award at our troop one evening long ago. I was told that, at the time, our troop had tied a national record for having the most Scouts receive Scouting's highest award at one ceremony. I have always been proud to be a part of that event and I still am.

The significance of the Eagle Scout Award, the programs of the Boy Scouts of America and my appreciation of all that Scouting in my youth had meant to me were all contributing factors in the way I immersed myself in the planning of the February Court of Honor. The planning for the event was an escape mechanism from my self-pity. I devoted so much time to the detailed planning and execution of this ceremony that, for a time, the business was completely out of my mind – THANK GOD!

Back in December I knew that there would be at least three Eagle Scouts for the award ceremony. I also knew that we, as a troop, were capable of doing even better. Every week from mid-December on, I would question those Scouts who were near to completion of their Eagle Scout rank how I could help them finish their requirements in time to receive their Eagle rank in February. All of these guys were moving along with their rank advancement requirements but seemed to lack a sense of urgency. I gathered those not yet finished with their requirements together and announced to them that I would meet with them at any time or place and under any circumstances to help them either individually or as a group complete their work for their Eagle Scout Rank advancement.

I began to call the six whose work was not complete at their home once a week. I suppose today I would go to jail for harassing these kids. As early January came, I began to call each Scout individually every evening to check on their progress. One evening as I was calling these guys, a call came to me between calls. One of these Scouts called and said, "This is the call you've been waiting for. I've finished all the requirements."

I asked, "Does this mean I can't harass you anymore?" The Scout said, "That's right – at least about my Eagle Scout rank anyway." He was right. This was the call I'd been waiting for.

Knowing we had the potential to have a number of Eagle Scouts in one ceremony, I wanted to make this event as special and memorable for these Scouts as I possibly could. There was only one man I wanted to invite to be our guest speaker and award presenter.

The National Offices of The Boy Scouts of America has an honor that is very seldom awarded. It is The Distinguished Eagle Scout Award. This recognition is presented only to individuals of outstanding character who have distinguished themselves in their careers, given of themselves for public betterment and earned their Eagle Scout Award at least 25 years ago. The award is rare and cannot be earned. After extensive research regarding the recipient and approval by a selection committee, it may only be granted by the national office based upon the recommendations of the local council office.

At the time, our local Chippewa Valley Council had only one such recipient of this award. They had chosen to bestow this most prestigious award on one of our areas circuit court judges. I hoped he would be available for our ceremony. This individual would give true class, dignity and real meaning to the presentation of these prestigious awards to these young men who had worked so hard to earn them. I wanted that dignity and class and felt that this was only fitting and much deserved by these fine young men.

I called the judge and he agreed to my request. I was thrilled to have secured such an outstanding example of what being an Eagle Scout is all about for this event.

I worked with our troop committee on the other details of the upcoming event. We planned out the entire event down to the most minor detail. I did whatever I could and then tried to do more. I wanted this ceremony to be the very best possible event of its kind for these young men. Besides, staying extremely busy planning the event, I wasn't allowing myself to wallow in the quagmire of my business situation. This was exactly the sort of mental release from the business that I so needed.

February 10th arrived. I spent most of the day setting up for the evening's event. Two of my assistant scoutmasters joined me to help make certain that the program would go on as smoothly as possible. We did a lot of checking and rechecking to make certain all was in order.

We had set 7:00 p.m. as the starting time for the ceremony. The scouts started to arrive around 6:30 p.m. I had set out all of the awards to be presented to the Scouts on a table in front of the room. What a beautiful sight that table was! The judge was not yet there at 6:55 and I was getting nervous. He is a terribly busy man and I hoped that he had not been called to other duties for the evening. Thank GOD, the judge arrived with three minutes to spare! This did not leave a whole lot of time for the judge and me to review his part in the Eagle Scout Award presentation ceremony.

I walked up to the podium at the front of the very crowded church basement room full of kids and their parents to welcome everyone to our February Court of Honor. We did all the traditional things at the beginning of these ceremonies – The Pledge of Allegiance, repeated the Scout Oath and the Scout Law, etc. All of the troop's adult staff members helped present rank advancements, awards and recognitions to the entry level Scouts and on up through the ascending ranks. Then it was time to call on the judge to speak to the group. After that, he would make the presentations of the Eagle Scout Awards.

The judge, with the red, white and blue ribbon around his neck with the suspended golden medallion of the Distinguished Eagle Scout

Award, walked up to the podium for his portion of the program. He spoke to the assemblage of responsibility, character, good citizenship and civic duty and how these characteristics were incumbent on these new Eagle Scouts. There he stood, this man of impeccable character, a highly respected community leader and a highly regarded public servant, speaking to this assembly of young people and their parents about the real true meaning of being an Eagle Scout. The entire room was silent while the judge spoke. All present heard every word he said.

Upon completion of his speech, I called seven fine young men and their parents to the front of the room. There each individual Scout, in their turn, was presented with the Eagle Scout Award he had earned by the Chippewa Valley Councils only Distinguished Eagle Scout. The judge pinned the Eagle Scout medallions on each Scout and individually congratulated each young man on his highly regarded and rare accomplishment. At the end of the ceremony, all seven Eagle Scouts had their picture taken with the judge. As a professional, he handled the ceremony with the dignity and class I knew he would.

The Court of Honor had been a wonderful evening for the all of he Scouts and their families as well as their scoutmaster who felt completely fulfilled at the end of the program. That night, after that ceremony, I could have dropped dead and felt completely satisfied with my life. I had focused all of my energy on making certain that this celebration of a rare accomplishments for these young men went off perfectly. I was so proud of these young men and their dedication to excellence. I was proud to be a scouting volunteer.

On that night and at that time in my life, I may not have had much of anything worthwhile going for me, but I did have that ceremony. I had successfully used my total involvement in that ceremony to block out any thoughts of my business predicament.

Never the less, a day later, I sank back into the old routine of feeling defeated, of feeling sorry for myself, of viewing a myself as a loser. Two old contractor friends of mine came to my rescue at time when I really needed them. We'll call them "Ron" and "Joe" for the purposes of this part of the story.

Ron, a local contractor whom I had worked with on several projects, called me to join him for a cup of coffee that Thursday morning following the Court of Honor. When we met, he began by saying that he hadn't seen me around the area in some time and wondered what I had been up to recently. It was curiosity which had caused him to call just because he hadn't heard or seen anything of me for well over a year.

I began to relate all of my problems to Ron (at which point I'm sure he was glad he had called me – yeh, right). He told me he had been in the same position except that he, perhaps, had even been in more trouble than I presently found my self in. In brief form, he shared with me how he had gone about reorganizing things after his "fall". He had to sell vehicles and equipment too.

He noted that when pricing equipment for sale, you need to be reasonable about it and don't expect to get pie-in-the-sky prices. If priced above market value, you will continue to lose value on the equipment while the interest on your loan just keeps on ticking as the equipment continues to sit in your yard. So set the price reasonably and get rid of the stuff ASAP. He told me where to advertise and in which publications to offer the equipment for the best results.

His coaching was much appreciated since there are really no manuals to tell you what to do when you're broke. Besides the good and much needed information, I came away from that morning coffee with Ron with a glimmer of hope and a shaky belief that I actually could walk up out of this mess. I had to laugh as we parted when he said to me, "During my lifetime and my career, I've gone BROKE and I've been divorced – I'd rather go BROKE!"

Early Friday morning, Joe, another area contractor, called inviting me to join him for breakfast. Like Ron, Joe's motivation for calling me was curiosity. As I began to relate my story to Joe, he only listened for a minute or two and then abruptly cut me off with these words of wisdom, "Look kid, your old man went BROKE a couple of times and went out a winner. So, now it's your turn. I'm going to tell you a couple things that your old man told me when I went down the first time and I didn't know what to do or where to turn. First, you ain't much of a contractor until you've gone BROKE a couple of times. Second, they can't eat ya." I started to laugh for the first time in a long time.

Then Joe began to relate a series of "war stories" about some area contractors and some of the largest contractors in the country who had, over their careers, hit bottom too. I probably embarrassed Joe, but by the time he was done with his rendition of some real hard luck stories and the stories of how these guys had rebounded from the bottom of the ladder, I was roaring with laughter which certainly felt good. Laughter had been missing in my life for a long time. It was probably Joe's delivery style which added so much humor to the series of stories he shared with me about overcoming failure to triumph in the end.

At the end our breakfast meeting, I thanked Joe for sharing his time and these stories of hope with me because I really needed this. As I left the café, I had two feelings. First, my stomach ached from laughing so much. Second, and more importantly, I had the feeling that I was capable of rebuilding the firm and getting on with my life and back in the game.

PLANNING THE WAY OUT

My sister and I had to come up with a plan to generate some working capital. We had no money and no work. Add to that, it wasn't snowing.

By late February, we were in default on our note at the bank.

We talked to our lawyer. He said he could "buy us" up to a year of keeping the bank off our backs without mentioning any of the details about how this would be made to happen. I guess he was talking about some form of bankruptcy proceedings. He indicated, there was no use digging into that possibility until the bank made the move we were dreading. He advised us to liquidate assets to keep the bank at bay. So, basically, he was repeating the idea I had already worked out with the bank.

Liquidating assets is a means of paying off debt. However, when *all* of your assets are pledged as collateral on the loan you want to pay down, in order to make those sales take place, you must obtain the banks blessing. If the bank should choose to "hold its ground" (not allow sales of assets to take place) you have two choices: wait for the bank to step in and sell off your assets (usually at a public auction) or declare bankruptcy. We did not care for either of these two options and fortunately, the bank was not interested in the auction option. That left us with selling our assets ourselves.

I asked for a meeting with Pete at the bank to discuss selling off some of our older vehicles and equipment at auction. I told Pete of an idea my sister had to have a "junk sale" auction to generate some working capital for the firm. We would clean out our storage sheds and sell off old stuff we never used anymore but the sort of stuff that contractors seem to accumulate over time. That was OK with Pete.

We worked out an agreement. The proceeds of any sale, either at this proposed auction or the direct sales of vehicles and equipment, as the bank had agreed to before, would be split 80/20. We would keep the 20% to be used as working capital to operate our business and the bank would receive 80% to pay back interest on the loan.

Without any cash, we went ahead with the "junk sale" auction.

My sister and I discussed signing the sod field over to the bank if such a move would satisfy the loan. Nothing lasts forever and our sod sales had been in steady decline for some time. Some area "up-start" landscape contractors had begun hauling sod into our area from the huge sod fields north of the metro-Twin Cities, Minnesota, area. The highly competitive market in this larger populated area of the Twin Cities had driven the price of sod down to the point where we could buy and haul the commodity for less that we could grow and harvest our own in our own field.

Another consideration to be kept in mind was the recent surge in industrial development around our sod field. Factories and warehouses were being built on the northeast side of Menomonie, Wisconsin, at a rapid pace. This industrial development made our sod field a very valuable piece of property if only we could sell it. We listed the property with a local realtor.

Many of our larger pieces of equipment were cleaned up, and parked in local equipment dealer's yard on a consignment basis. The thinking here was that equipment buyers look for equipment in dealer's yards when thinking of making a purchase. Equipment buyers don't look in contractor's yards so why not place the equipment where equipment buyers usually go shopping. If the dealers sold the equipment, we would pay a commission but we felt that the commission would be worth the price charged since our chances of making the much-needed sales were so much better.

This thinking made sense and actually worked out quite well. In dealer's yards, equipment seemed to take on more of a legitimacy, an air of genuine sales worthiness and sound mechanical correctness. Parked in a contractor's yard, machinery is too often viewed as used junk regardless of its mechanical condition. Then too, construction equipment without contractor's logo decals becomes very generic. It is judged not by who owned it last, but by what condition it appears to be in at the time. Although this is a mind game of sorts, it worked and it worked well.

Selling this equipment was killing me on a personal level. Over time I had become so captivated in materialism and all the baggage that goes along with this thinking. I viewed my worth as a human being by the things and stuff I had gathered around me. I became so enamored with materialism that I would rather study a set of plans and read a "spec book" than read a novel. It was by bidding bigger and bigger projects (provided that these projects were profitable) that I was able to buy more and bigger and better machinery and trucks. Besides my expanded fleet of equipment, my business acumen and reputation were growing as well which further fueled my materialism. Now, because of this materialism, each machine or vehicle I sold, I viewed as a loss of personal self-worth. It was as though, well, there goes a part of me.

I had worked so hard and taken so many risks to attain the level of business I had achieved before going broke. Taking the risks had always allowed me to purchase bigger, better and newer machinery and trucks. I viewed these acquisitions as tangible evidence that I was of more importance and of more worth as a person. Looking back on it now, ultimately, it was materialism which was driving me.

Vehicles and machines started to sell and sell at good prices, but these sales were just taking me lower. Despite that, when I would take the sales receipts to the bank for deposit, I would always try to meet with Pete to show him how we were doing with sales. I would bring in trade publications showing the same model and vintage truck or machine with the listed price of that item and then show him what we had received when selling ours. Consistently, we got higher prices for our equipment than the advertised prices in the trade journals. Pete was happy with our results.

Equipment liquidation and cash flow from small but profitable jobs held the bank at bay for a year but we were really not yet winning. We simply weren't making a lot of progress in getting ahead of our tremendous debt load. In a business sense, we were just "treading water" at best.

SALVATION SALE

The key to ending our company's financial dilemma was the liquidation of the sod field land in Menomonie, Wisconsin. The sod farm had been listed for over a year with a Menomonie based realty firm. There were only a couple of casual inquiries but no serious offers other than a few would-be thieves. The real-estate firm we had listed the property with was not getting the job done. We ended that relationship. The bank, though held at bay for about a year, was getting nervous and hinted they were ready to pounce.

Now, what to do?

My sister and I thought of every individual we knew in western Wisconsin who would possibly have the money, or the borrowing power or guts enough to purchase what was definitely becoming a rather "hot" piece of property. We sent them all letters and a map of the property noting its location.

I used a plot map of the land and marked out the close proximity of the land to the I-94/County Trunk "B" exit at exit 45. I also indicated on the plan the location of property directly across the road from our property that Wal-Mart had just purchased. They were going to build a 70-acres-under-roof distribution center. Wal-Mart needed 200 contiguous acres to accommodate all of the truck parking around their facility. We only had 70 acres but ours abutted I-94. Had we owned more acreage, I'm sure they would have been the buyers of our property. The map also indicated that our land was adjacent to the City of Menomonie Industrial Park property. The sod field was practically surrounded by "hot property".

One of the people on my list was an old customer of ours with whom we'd done a lot of business over the years. He was a well-connected realtor and developer. I explained that we were trying to sell the sod farm to get out from under our debt load. We needed to move fast to get the bank off our back before they sold us out.

From our past dealings with the realtor/developer, I knew I could trust his judgment and that he would keep our conversation confidential. I showed him one of my maps. He took one look at the plan and said, "There's only one logical buyer for that piece of property and that's the City of Menomonie. Tell you what I'll do. Since you're in trouble, I'll work for you by the hour charging you a consulting fee only. When we make the deal to sell the land, I won't charge you a commission. You can't afford to pay a commission, so I won't charge you other than for my time as your consultant. I'll need to call your banker and I'll make a few other phone calls yet today to get the ball rolling. I'll stay in touch with you on this." Interestingly, there was no "if" as far as he was concerned about this land sale which I really appreciated hearing at that time. He was just the sort of "go-getter" we needed at the time!

Within a week, I received a phone call from the realtor/developer about having a meeting with the City Manager of the City of Menomonie. The Mayor would also be at the meeting. They were interested in discussing the purchase of the sod farm acreage for the expansion of the industrial park.

We met. After I introduced myself, the realtor did all the talking. The Mayor and the City Manager said they would propose the deal to the City Council at the next council meeting. They would get back to us after the council discussed the proposal. I tried not to show it but I was ecstatic. I hoped that the Mayor and the City Manager were not poker players because I knew I had probably let my guard down on my poker face.

The city council was not going to meet for two weeks and time was running out with the bank. I was anxious about getting the deal completed sooner but I really could not express that point to the city representatives. I did share this with the realtor on our drive back to Eau Claire after the meeting.

"Don't worry", he said, "we'll have a deal and it will be in time to keep the bank happy – DONT WORRY!"

I just couldn't be worry free. I was nervous about the timing of the deal. Schedules were just too tight, too close for me to feel comfortable about anything.

Within two weeks, the realtor and I were back in the Menomonie City Hall for a meeting with the City Manager, His Honor the Mayor and a few members of the City Council as well as Industrial Development Committee people. Their purchase proposal was ready for our review. In total amount, the offer was somewhat less than the surrounding property was selling for at the present time. The realtor did all the talking. Basically, he expressed to the gathering that we wanted to study the proposal and that we would get back to the city officials in one week. Since I'm certain that at times I can be "read like a book", I'm convinced that I looked as sick as I felt.

This time as we drove back to Eau Claire, I began to ask about the reasonableness of the proposed deal the city was offering. If we could just hold on a little longer, I noted, we could get substantially more for the property. Afterall, we knew what Wal-Mart had paid per acre for the property they acquired on the other side of the road and the city's offer was not close to that amount. Being the gentleman that he is, the realtor offered to try to market the land to other potentially interested groups who deal in speculative land acquisition. He went on to say that these speculators notoriously pay rock bottom prices for properties they know they will need to "sit on" for a time in order to make a profit from the sale of the land.

When we arrived back at our office, the realtor reviewed the city's proposal with my sister and we all discussed the matter further. The realtor and I shared with my sister the facts about the price paid by Wal-Mart as opposed to the price offered by the city. Neither my sister nor I were happy with the deal as presented. We asked if he thought a counter proposal would be a good idea. The advice was really what neither of us wanted to hear.

The realtor began, "Well, you have an offer on the table from the only really logical purchaser of the property. I know you are not happy with this proposal. I could try to market this property for you to investor groups or you could simply list the property and pray that someone buys it in time to save you from your bank. That's the choice you two will need to make. My advice to both of you is this. The deal that is presently being offered to you will get the job done in terms of the bank. I've checked this out and I know this to be true. I would not suggest a counter offer of any terms or conditions or price because I would not want to see you lose the deal that will save your company. That being said, you have my advice but you have to make the decision. I can't. It's your property. Let me know what you want to do. I'll be in my office. In terms of the price others are getting for their property, you can dream all you want, then there's the reality and there is the bank.

We were facing the biggest decision of our lives. In truth, there really was no choice. Only the accepting nod was left to us.

We nodded.

The deal was done one week later at the Menomonie City Hall. The proceeds from the sale went to the bank. The bank held the balance due back to our firm until all of the paperwork surrounding the full satisfaction of the note was completed by the bank. As a result of the cash surrendered to the bank from the land sale, we no longer faced the possibility of being sold out by the bank. We had satisfied our notes. Though still without much cash, and still in debt but at a much lesser amount, we were no longer facing the certain death of our business. While we were not yet completely free of the bank's hand, we were no longer in the dangerous situation we had been not too long ago.

The "frosting on the cake" happened two months later. Our neighbors, for whom we had built the back nine holes of their golf course several years before, refinanced their debt on their golf course. At the time we had built the "back-nine" for them, they were unable to pay for the work. Our firm financed that project just to try to keep our crews busy during the economic downturn. As a result of the neighbors refinancing, they paid off their note to our firm including every penny of interest. That payment from them put a substantial pile of cash in our company's checkbook.

Upon receipt of the check from our neighbors, my sister called Pete at the bank and asked him to get all of the paperwork ready because she was going to come to the bank to pay off our loans completely.

"Pete's response, "NO SHIT? - REALLY?" (That's kind of banker.)

"Really", she said.

After a long, terrible ordeal, our firm was debt free and we had adequate operating capital once again.

I had gone BROKE. I had become a human wreck and generally dropped out of the business scene while feeling sorry for myself and wasting years of my life. After this salvation sale of the sod field and then the unexpected income from our neighbors, the firm was no longer broke. Both my human and my business spirit were restored - unbroken again. I was ready to have another go at life and a have another go at business as well. With this renewed zest for life and a regenerated enthusiasm for business, both of which I had lost after my dream job, I was looking forward to my next opportunity, whatever it may be.

PART VI - MID-LIFE DO-OVER

BACK IN THE GAME

All of 1991, 1992, and the first few months of 1993 were wasted feeling sorry for myself. I was unable to focus on business because I was focused on my failure and I couldn't seem to get away from dwelling on that.

My sister and I had been limping along in business since my disaster at Lutsen taking on smaller landscaping and grading jobs in the area – nothing big. After we returned the business to some sort of normal, I was not doing all that I should have to help restore things to pre-business catastrophe conditions. My heart was really never in lawns and shrubbery. I liked machinery and trucks and earth moving and sculpting and grading. The truth is, I had a passion for the intricacies involved in the building of golf courses.

It was during this time that my sister announced she was getting married. She had met a guy who was back in western Wisconsin visiting his mother. He was living in Denver, Colorado, at that time. They decided that they wanted to live out in Colorado so it was decided that we would split the business. She would get the Alpine Landscape Canter building and grounds and I would get the old shops and surrounding property. Her half was worth a little more than mine, so I acquired a little cash as we split the business – just enough to start over if given the opportunity.

As early April of 1993 arrived, I received a phone call which would change everything. This phone call was the first of several stars which fell into alignment that spring. The cash was another.

My scout troop had been traveling to Galena, Illinois, for a number of years to participate in a gathering of upper-mid-western states scouts. The Blackhawk Area Council of the Boy Scouts of America (northwestern Illinois) hosts an annual event on the last weekend of April. Galena, Illinois, is where U.S. Grant was living when President Lincoln called him up to lead the Union Army in the Civil War. The last Weekend of April is when Grant's birthday takes place and so the event is entitled the U.S. Grant Pilgrimage. Thousands of scouts and scouters from several states participate and have all sorts of scouting fun in Galena every year.

Each year, on our trip down to Galena, we would pass by the Galena Country Club on our way into the city. For several years, once the scouts became involve in the various events under the watchful eyes of my other adult leaders, I would travel back out to the golf course to hand out business cards and talk with some of the club members. In my scout uniform, I stood out like "a petunia in the onion patch". I always referred to this business promoting as "planting seeds". You just never know when one will sprout.

The phone call in mid-April was from the president of the Galena Country Club. "Are you still a golf course building contractor?"

"Yes!", I replied (though I had nothing other than my experience at the time – no machinery, equipment, vehicles or crew.)

"We would like to meet with you.", said the president.

"Certainly! I'll be there in a couple of weeks for the scouting event unless we need to meet earlier.", I shot back.

"No, that will be fine. We want to add a nine-hole addition to our course and we remembered you and would like to have you take a look at the project when you are here.", he said.

WOW!

While attending the U.S. Grant pilgrimage, I left the scouts with other adult leaders to meet with several of the members of the board of directors and the president of the Galena Country Club on Saturday afternoon. I supplied them with my resume and my credentials list, a listing of the golf courses I had built along with contact phone numbers to call for references. We toured the site for the proposed nine-hole addition during which time I took a lot of notes concerning each hole individually, based on the plan they had at that time. After touring the layout, we went back to the clubhouse to talk over their plans, thoughts and ideas.

At the time of this meeting, they didn't really have a golf course construction plan. All they really had was a "routing plan" which denoted centers of greens, centers of tees, dog-leg swing points, distances of holes in terms of length of play in yardage and not much more.

"Could I work with something so basic or did I need more detailed drawings?", I was asked.

This was an ideal opportunity in that I could propose a design/build project.

"I can work this project with just what you have at present," I replied. "I can field design the greens, tees and sand traps because I've built hundreds of these features before. In addition, I can build these features to "fit the land" thereby keeping earthmoving costs low. I know what to look for in terms of where and how to locate these features from past experience."

"On the other hand," I continued, "If you would like to spend more money on a more complete set of plans, certainly you can do this. Or, we can use the money you save by not spending any more on design work and drawings and put that money towards better uses in building better, more interesting and more aesthetically pleasing design features. I'll be happy to work with you either way. Let me know how you would like to proceed."

They decided on the spot.

"If you feel comfortable with the plans we have, please give us a price to do the work. What you have proposed sounds good.", they said.

I replied, "I'll be happy to price the project and I'll call so we can set up a meeting to review and discuss my proposal. I will answer any questions you may have concerning your project or my past projects. I would only ask that when we meet, you have a local earthmoving contractor at the meeting so we could get acquainted because I intend to work with local contractors for supply of project materials and construction services."

I drove back into downtown Galena to get back with my scout troop for the balance of the Saturday activities. We arose Sunday morning, enjoyed breakfast, packed our camping gear and belongings and headed for home. This Galena trip, for the old Scoutmaster, had been wonderful in two ways. The scouts had a lot of fun as they do every year at this activity plus, I had "set the hook."

On Monday morning, I began to work up the pricing for the Galena project. I spent a couple of days reviewing notes, figuring quantities of materials needed and developing a proposal. I called the president of the golf club and we set a meeting date and time.

In the mean-time, the president and members of the board, based on my credentials list, drove north to New Glarus, Wisconsin, the project I had done which was closest in proximity to theirs. Thank GOD, they chose that project because the folks at New Glarus loved me. Better yet, that golf course was my first design/build project.

We met and, sure enough, they had invited an earthmoving contractor who could also supply the sand and other materials needed for the project. The contractor and I got along well and he furnished me with materials prices and machinery hourly rental rates - all of which fit my proposal perfect.

The Board of Directors and I reviewed the project and my proposal. They gave me the "go ahead" right then and there. I said I would go back home and have my attorney draw up the contract. They and their attorney could review the contract documents and, if all was found to be in order, they could sign it, include the down-payment check and return it to me. We would begin to move equipment to Galena the day after receiving the signed contract and the check.

I had my attorney set the contract up in such a way that each element of the job was individually priced. Inspections were to happen every thirty days. Using this elemental method, each teeing surface, each sand trap, each green cavity was *unit priced"*, which is to say so much per element completed. In my previous experience, wherein I had little or no control of the payments I sought, golf course construction bidding had always been *"lump sum"*, meaning the entire project will cost so much. Based on this lump sum, payments to the contractor were determined on a percentage of completion of the entire project by the designer (think back to the previously mentioned mess at Amery, Wisconsin).

To avoid all of this percentages of completion confusion which included a couple of tough instances in the past where payments were delayed, unit pricing on this project, like New Glarus, was straight forward. Either the teeing surface is built or it is not. Either the green cavity is shaped or it is not. Either the tile lines in the floor of the greens are installed or they are not. The same with the greens floor gravel bed over the tile lines. The same with the "greens mix" placed in the green's cavity. Sand trap shaped. Sand in the trap. Elemental. Either a golf hole is seeded or it is not. No negotiations, no guess-work and no "foggy areas". Everything was straight forward.

But the major thing in this contract, like New Glarus, was that acceptance was mandated to be done on a hole-by-hole basis. By contractual language, when any given golf hole was completed and accepted by the club, that acceptance was final. From then on, that hole was totally *their responsibility* and no longer *mine*. The weather could get as foul as it wanted to because after final acceptance, any erosion damage and repair was no longer *my* problem.

I had learned from my dream job. I thought about my previous debacle at Lutsen long and hard. On that project and others before, I had to turn over to the owners of the project a totally completed golf course - all 9 or all 18 holes at one time. This meant in essence that, as the contractor, I was guaranteeing the weather for the entire time it took to complete the project in order that the whole thing was ready for final inspection in one fell swoop.

Foul weather conditions during completion process had destroyed me at Lutsen. I was no longer willing to take that chance. That is why I had my attorney include this language about the finality of acceptance on a hole-by-hole basis in the contract. I had had enough of guaranteeing the weather.

As promised, we moved machinery into Galena the day after the signed contract and the down-payment were received. I called a number of my former crew members to find out about their employment status. Some were available and I hired them right away. It's hard to find experienced people. We went right to work and launched into the project. Our "native" contractor/supplier was a pleasure to work with on the project. We'd never worked with any better.

For the Galena project, I rented the machinery I needed to do the job. After the job at Lutsen, I thought about machinery ownership at length and having to sell nearly everything we owned as well. I lived and worked in the northern tier of states which afforded me roughly eight months of weather in which to work. Then of course, there were the rain days followed by soil conditions that were too muddy to even dream of making progress on projects. In realistic terms, I had roughly 160 – 180 days in which operate machinery to make a living. No matter that limited time frame, the "easy monthly payments" and the interest on equipment purchase programs goes on 365 days per year. If one looks at things in a realistic light, perhaps renting is a better way to go.

Though it was an unusually rainy year, we never-the-less progressed on the project very well throughout the summer. I was glad that we had the hole-by-hole acceptance clause in the contract. Throughout the entire project, we never had any disputes whatsoever about completion of any of the elements of the work. We finished the project completely in early October. The project was profitable and I was back.

There was only one "dark cloud" hanging over that business season and it wasn't a rain cloud. This thing was worse.

WANNABEES ATTACK

That fall, just prior to project completion in Galena, I had an unusual occurrence happen to me one week when we were rained out on the job. Since the project site was a muddy, saturated mess, I drove home to catch up on some local business and get some office work completed. When I pulled into the yard at the shop, there was a car parked close to the building. A guy got out of the car whom I recognized from somewhere in the past. I got out of my vehicle and walked toward him. He was smiling and asked how I was doing.

While he made this small talk, I was trying to figure out what this was all about. Then I found out the real reason for his visit. He said, "Sorry about this". He handed me some papers after which he hurriedly got in his car and left. I opened the papers and found that he had just served me a summons and complaint. The good folks at the golf course I had worked on in Duluth, Minnesota, several years ago were suing me!

As previously mentioned, this is the job where I had been lied to about the golf club's finances. I never got paid on that job for 90 days because, in truth, they never had their finances in order until that time. We had started the project in good faith, but after being unable to collect for the work we were accomplishing, I began to reduce the crew numbers on the job. I sent these operators and other workmen to other projects I had underway at the time. I did keep up my end of the contract by never totally abandoning the job. I left a "skeleton crew" there and working every day.

Finally collecting for work completed after 90 days, I bolstered the crew and we really got a lot of work done in a short time period. However, due to delays caused by their lack of honesty, we finished the job very late in the season. At that late date, the ground temperature was too cold for the grass seeds to germinate.

The following spring, the Duluth area was inundated with rainstorms. This caused erosion on the golf course since there was no standing turf grass to hold the soils on the slopes. Apparently, the rain storms and the unsprouted turf grasses were my fault.

I had never been sued before. I thought about this and figured that if I was being sued in Minnesota, I needed a Minnesota based and licensed lawyer to represent me. The only one I knew was a lawyer who had been a member of the board of directors at the Deerwood project. I called, made an appointment and drove to his office. We'll call him "Mike" for this story.

Once there, I showed him the paperwork and briefly discussed my problem.

Mike said, "You've never been sued before, have you?"

"NO! - Never!", I replied.

"Well, I appreciate you thinking of me to represent you. However, you really don't need me. What you need to do is to call your insurance company. You have contractor's liability insurance and they, your insurance company, will provide legal counsel for you and your little problem. You've already paid for this through your insurance premiums. But thanks for thinking of me.", Mike concluded.

I told Mike that it has always been my practice to keep a journal, a log book of sorts, and make a daily journal entry on each and every project I ever did. An old contractor had advised me to make this a practice. He told me having his project journal as evidence in the courtroom had saved him from going **BROKE** on a major project he had done years ago.

Typically, either my project superintendents or I made daily journal entries at the end of each working day on every project. Noted in the journal were weather conditions, soil conditions, man and machine assignments, problems and solutions to problems encountered the previous day. Entries also included progress of the work for that day and other factors which would give clarity to how the project was moving through the time line of the job. The only problem on the Duluth job was that my superintendent quit to take another job and took the project journal with him when he left or threw it away or…

So, at a time when I really needed a specific project journal, I didn't have the only one which would back up the chronology of events on that particular job. I had a project journal for every other project I had ever worked, but not this one in Duluth - the only one I ever really needed. I had no clear day-by-day notes to back up my defense. I had nothing.

Mike said this, "I don't give a damn what you are presently doing or involved in at this time. Forget that for now. You go back home, sit down at your desk and write down every little thing, every detail, every event, every occurrence that you can recall surrounding your Duluth job. I don't care if this process takes you an entire week. Write everything you can remember down on paper. Start on this just as soon as you can. Be very diligent about this. Begin thinking about this on your way home and make some mental notes. At this point in time there is really nothing more important in your life than remembering and writing down as much of this stuff about that project as you can. Oh, by the way, I won't bill you for my time, I'll just call this a little friendly advice".

Lucky me! I thanked Mike and left for the long drive home.

During the drive home, I thought a lot about that project in Duluth. It's strange all those details you can remember if you concentrate on the things that went on before, during and after that project.

Now back at home, I called my insurance agent and told him about the series of events that had taken place in the last few days. He informed me that he would get in touch with the insurance company and that I could expect a phone call shortly from corporate headquarters.

A long phone conversation followed with the corporate office's man about what had taken place on the job. He told me that I would be hearing from an attorney in Duluth very soon so that we could "put a case together" and "get the ball rolling" on this thing ASAP.

Not too long after hanging up from the corporate man I received a phone call from a Duluth based attorney. We'll call him "Steve".

I told Steve about how little I knew about being sued. I then shared with him what Mike had told me about writing down everything I could remember about the job in Duluth. Steve told me that I had received priceless advice from Mike and that I should carry through with that process. When finished with that, I should call him to set up an appointment so we could meet face-to-face. I was to bring my notebook of project recollections with me. Of course, this meeting would take place at his offices in Duluth.

It was rather unnerving driving to Duluth and all the while thinking of how his lawsuit could, more or less, end my career as a golf course builder. Solicitations for golf course construction are based on the reputation and resume of contractors being invited to either bid or submit proposals for projects. With a black blotch on one's reputation, opportunities would certainly dwindle if not disappear altogether.

Once in Duluth, after the ride to the top floor of the office building, I met Steve. He invited me into his very plush, well decorated office. It was immediately evident that I was not dealing with a "second stringer" It was obvious this guy was a "big-leaguer". We had a sit-down chat. He took me to lunch at a very historic, high-end, exclusive men's club downtown. Everything was first class. During lunch we continued our chat about the project.

Back in his office, discussion about the project continued once again. Being located in the city where this construction job had gone on, Steve had "heard things" and assured me that he knew a number of the people involved. Steve went on to explain that the City of Duluth had two municipal golf courses and two private golf clubs – one, a real up-scale links, for the wealthier locals and one for local wannabees. My work had been done at the wannabees golf course.

He asked me to hand over the notebook I had just completed. He wanted to study the contents and set up a plan of action for the trial including scheduling depositions from a number of the characters involved in the project. He sent me back home and said he'd be in touch.

Meanwhile, we finished our project in Galena and were paid promptly. Winter was setting in and I hadn't heard a word from Steve in some time. He called in mid-January. Could I be at his office the following day to begin the depositions process? Certainly.

Winter in Duluth, Minnesota, must be experienced to be understood. Located on the western end of Lake Superior, Duluth is very beautiful, picturesque city but very brutal during the winter months. Winter winds are endlessly howling off the world's largest body of freshwater. Winter is one thing with low, low temperatures, but combine those low temperatures with the wind and you have *windchill temperatures* in the double digits below zero. To say that these windchill temperatures are nasty is to make a gross understatement. Driving north to Duluth during the winter months, one only hopes that the vehicle you are driving doesn't freeze up in that sub-zero weather. I made it, but the trip north was an ordeal.

Depositions are no fun. The plaintiff's attorney team was there in Steve's office to grill me about a number of things on their minds. It is interesting the way lawyers frame their questions and then ask the very same question using different wordage but always seeking he same answer. I'm certainly no lawyer, but how dumb did they think I was? When they didn't get the response to the question they were seeking, they'd have another "go" or two at the same issue. So much of this was just so silly. I would characterize much of the deposition procedure as "word games" or "word-craft" in an attempt to confuse or frustrate the person being deposed. They use what are called leading questions because they intend to lead the deposed to entrapment. That's the way this game was played. Get the person in the "hot seat" to give two or more differing answers to the same reworded question was the idea. What a sham.

Lawyers, being lawyers, tend to drag things out. The deposition part of the pre-trial setup seemed to go on forever. A phone call here, a letter there, depositions from all sorts of folks even in different areas of the country. It just goes on and on. To depose one witness, Steve even had to travel to Las Vegas, Nevada, to get this one character on record (This witness had moved out to Las Vegas from Duluth after the project was completed).

Spring of 1994 arrived. I had negotiated a nine-hole golf course expansion project in Mora, Minnesota. We were well underway in Mora when the Duluth project court case came to trial.

Without a doubt, the week of the trial spent in Duluth, Minnesota, was one of the worst weeks of my life. I will say it was interesting but the mental pressure was horrific. Steve had me living in a luxury hotel in downtown Duluth about a block from the St. Louis County Courthouse. I brought all of the records I had having to do with the job. Fortunately, I had the crewmembers time cards so I could piece together much of the project even though I didn't have the project journal. But so much of the information contained in the journals have to do with weather and soil conditions, recorded daily progress, etc. I didn't have what I really needed but I would have to make do with what I did have.

Before the trial began on Monday morning, the plaintiff's lawyer, Steve and I, the architect and his lawyer were to meet with His Honor, the judge, in chambers. He wanted to see if an agreement could be worked out among the parties involved in this dispute before going to trial. The judge asked if there could be a settlement to see to it that the trial would not go forward. I was absolutely shocked when Steve said to the gathered assemblage, "I have been authorized by my client's insurance company to write a check in amount of $250,000.00 to settle this matter."

The lawyer for the architect said nothing (I'm guessing the architect had no liability insurance). Why the architect was being sued, I have no idea, other than the plaintiff's lawyer just wanted to include him in the party.

The judge looked at the plaintiff's lawyer who responded, "No way! We want the whole thing – we want the entire $750,000.00"!

I wondered where on earth they had come up with such an amount to compensate for the alleged damages they allegedly had suffered.

The judge then asked the plaintiff's attorney how long he planned to take to try this dispute. The response was, "All week long. I've got many witnesses to be heard by the jury."

Jury selection was next. I was amazed that the selected jury members were all women and not one in the entire lot was a golfer.

The actual trial started about an hour before lunch break when the first witness was called to the stand to testify. Then lunch. Then witness after witness after witness and on and on for the next four and a half days. It was less than fun having to sit there listening to the witnesses who were all there to testify that you, the defendant, knew absolutely nothing whatsoever about golf course construction. Your methods, proper techniques to do each and every element of the project, and your work overall was substandard or incorrect or incomplete. In addition, you were egregiously negligent in the performance of your obligations under the terms and conditions of the contract.

Steve prepared me for this. He said, "No matter what is said about you, your firm, your crewmembers and the work that you did, you sit there with the total poker-face and *do not* flinch, grimace or make any sort of movement that would indicate your discomfort! Just sit there and take it no matter how false or dishonest or just plain goofy the adverse statements about you and your work really are. Just sit there and take it stone-faced. Don't flinch!"

Well now, listing to many of the allegations, that was really tough to do. But I did as I was instructed because I knew I had to do so.

One of the plaintiff's key witnesses was a Doctor Robert --------, PhD. from some prestigious east coast university. The plaintiffs had flown this witness to Duluth to inspect the project and then testify as their expert witness based on his expertise, education and notoriety. It took at least fifteen, maybe twenty minutes just to read off Dr. Robert --------'s resume and credentials. He had authored a bookshelf of books on various subjects concerning turfgrass and proper fertilization, cures for insect infestations, turfgrass diseases and cures, chemical application, mowing techniques and proper golf course maintenance. The doctor was an expert in agronomy as well as entomology and horticulture. It was an impressive resume, to say the least.

The plaintiff's attorney was first up with Dr. Robert ------, PhD. Asking Doctor Robert-------, PhD. a few "milk toast" questions about his background as a nationally renowned turf grass specialist, he was always addressed as Doctor ---------. For instance:

"Doctor-------, is it your opinion that, after having observed the golf course here in question, the finishing and the seeding portion of the project was properly completed?', asked the plaintiff's lawyer.

The doctor's response, "Definitely not! It's terrible!"

"And continuing on, Doctor -------, based on what you saw after touring the project, did you find the sort of adequate turfgrass thickness one should expect on a project such as this?"

The doctor's response, "Not even close! It was terrible! Totally inadequate!"

"Well then Doctor -------, is it your professional opinion that the work performed on this project was of the level of workmanship one should expect from a golf course construction professional on a project such as this?", asked the plaintiff's lawyer.

The doctor's response, (naturally), "Unconscionable! No professional golf course builder would do such a haphazard, sloppy work!"

The plaintiff's attorney asked, "Doctor -------, again, in your professional opinion, what steps should have been taken which would have generated the sort of finished turfgrass surfaces normally found on golf course features similar to those found on this course?"

The doctor's response, as expected from previous responses - everything was way wrong, inadequate, poor workmanship, lacked professionalism, no finesse, bad practices employed, incompetence and on and on and on.

Every question directed at this highly acclaimed professional, this nationally recognized expert witness by the plaintiff's attorney, was always directed to Doctor--------. Always! This treatment was pure theatrics to emphasize the importance, the education, the vast knowledge, and the unquestionable authority, not to mention absolute, beyond questionable correctness of any and all responses by this scholarly and celebrated expert witness.

It was intimidating for me listening to the doctor repeatedly describing my incompetence. I was shaken though I couldn't show it per Steve's instructions. I'm thinking, who could possibly argue with this guy's testimony?

Now it was Steve's turn with Doctor Robert-------, PhD.

Steve asked, "Hey Bob, (notice - no Dr. Robert --------, PhD. here and Doctor Robert--------, PhD was obviously insulted and offended by Steve's manner of questioning and lack of respect for this highly acclaimed witness) Have you ever loaded a bale of mulch into a hydro-mulcher?"

The response, "Well, no."

Steve again, "Ever blended the guar into the hydro-mulch emulsion, Bob? And if so, what do you recommend for the blend ratio of guar to the emulsion in pounds per gallon?"

The response, "Well, no. I have no idea what you are talking about."

And again, "Well then, Bob, you certainly have held on to the spry cannon on a hydro-mulcher to apply the hydro-mulch emulsion on slopes then haven't you, Bob?"

The response, "Well, no."

Steve, "So then Bob, you're a big-time turf expert but you've never actually done any real-world work."

"OBJECTION!", yelled the plaintiff's lawyer.

"Overruled", said the judge, "The witness will answer the question."

The response, "Well no, my work has been in the laboratory"

Steve comes back again, "So then Bob, would it be fair to say that you know your way around the laboratory but you actually know very little about turfgrass where most turfgrasses actually grow?"

Silence. A blank stare from the good Doctor Robert--------, PhD.

At this point the plaintiff's attorney jumped to his feet and screeching, "OBJECTION!" and to Dr. Robert --------, "You don't have to answer that!"

The plaintiff's attorney was actually correct. Doctor Robert--------, PhD didn't have to answer the question - the damage had already been done.

Steve had demolished this expert witness in short order! This professional witness, this heavily credentialed expert who was always addressed as Dr. Robert ------- by the plaintiff's attorney was just plain old Bob in Steve's hands. The way Steve handled his interrogation of Bob, this witnesses credibility to testify in this case was simply ripped to shreds. It took Steve less than five minutes to accomplish this. When Steve got through with him, Dr. Robert -------, PhD. might just as well have stayed at home on the east coast.

After four and a half days of hearing of my incompetence, lack of professionalism, inexperience, poor workmanship, disregard for the plans and specifications, general stupidity and a host of other less than favorable attributes, lunch on Friday and the final escape from the courtroom was a welcome treat. Steve and I ate lunch together, as usual. This time Steve was grooming me because on this final afternoon of the trial, I was going to be the last guy in the witness stand. Well, of course, I was nervous. So, I said to Steve, "Well at least, you will get the final round of questioning."

Steve said, "Oh no. I go first. The plaintiff's attorney gets to do the final round of questioning." I sank. Steve went on, "Don't worry, you'll do just fine." Steve may well have been confident, I was not.

I was on the witness stand for at least an hour and a half being grilled by two attorneys – mine first and theirs last. Finally, after what seemed like an eternity, I was allowed to step down from the witness stand. I was exhausted.

Allegations had been made throughout the trial by any number of witnesses through the clever questioning by the plaintiff's attorney that the project was incomplete when we moved off the job. This was *the* major point in their case. Throughout the trial, the plaintiff's main focus had been to establish this argument to substantiate their claim of wrong-doing on my part. And, of course, my wrong-doing justified the outrageous compensation they were seeking based on my alleged failure to finish the project before leaving the jobsite. Indeed, the plaintiff's attorney's final statement was that the project was incomplete at the time we left the jobsite based on the testimony of a whole multitude of witnesses whom he listed off just to refresh the memories of the jury.

Then I witnessed a miracle…

What Steve did in the closing arguments stage of the trial was beyond belief.

"Incomplete? Not so!" said Steve, "My client completed the project in its entirety and I have indisputable proof! After this statement, HE RAISED THE DEAD (figuratively speaking) TO TESTIFY ON MY BEHALF AT THIS TRIAL!

As it happened, during construction, the golf club's representative, for contractual purposes, was the owner of a civil engineering firm in Duluth. It was up to this man to "sign off" on the project in conjunction with the golf course architect to determine the percentage of completion of the work which, of course, determined payments to be made to the contractor - me. In the time lapsed from the completion of the project to this trial, this man had passed away. Obviously, he couldn't be called on as a witness. However, Steve raised him from his grave, figuratively, to testify on my behalf.

Steve stated, "Though this witness could not be with us to testify today, we actually have proof that the club's representative knew that the project was 100% complete when my client moved off the job."

With that, Steve went over to his front of the courtroom table and produced exhibit # 32. This was a blown-up version of an American Institutes of Architects form entitled "Application and Certificate for Payment" signed and dated by the golf course architect, myself *and the deceased* certifying that the project was 100% complete, there was zero balance due and it was notarized.

Steve said to the jury and the others in attendance in the courtroom while pointing at the blow-up, "Look at this. Even though he couldn't be here with us today, here, on the date noted on this form, we have the signature of this State of Minnesota Licensed Professional Civil Engineer who fully knew and understood this AIA form. He understood what a 100% completed project meant and certified by his signature on the date noted on this form, that my client had fulfilled every part of his responsibilities concerning the project and the work involved in bringing this job to its conclusion. His signature is right here – and here is the date. See - look right here!"

WOW!

I know I was and I'm sure everybody else in the courtroom was totally flabbergasted hearing and seeing this presentation figuratively bringing the dead back to life! What an astonishing attorney!

The trial came to its conclusion late that Friday afternoon. The judge gave his instructions to the jury members and dismissed the jury to their jury chamber for deliberation. Steve said to me, "Look, this ain't Perry Mason. Nobody is going to jail. This is just about money. The jury has seven days in which to make their determination of the case so you may as well drive home. I'll give you a call when the jury decides. Who knows how long this process might take?"

I shook Steve's hand and thanked him for all that he had done. Not at all sure or confident of the outcome of the trial, I walked those frigid winter streets of Duluth one last time to my pickup and headed for home. This had been quite an ordeal.

Driving that 180 miles back to Eau Claire was torturous for me. All I could think about was; THERE GOES MY REPUTATION AS A GOLF COURSE BUILDER AND CONTRACTOR. I'M FINISHED IF THIS GOES THE WRONG WAY. How many days would I have to endure this mental anguish before I learned of the results? And then, if the outcome was against me, now what would I do for a living?

When I arrived at home after three grueling hours of winter driving, my wife had taped a big banner on the garage door. It read; YOU WON!

When I went in the house, my wife informed me that she had received a phone call some time back from Steve. He told her that the jury deliberated and found in our favor and that he'd call Monday so he and I could talk this over!

OH MY GOD!

That Monday Steve called and said, "I wish I could have known how this would go down. Had I known what was going to go on, I'd have asked you to stay in Duluth. The jury found in our favor after only twenty minutes of deliberation. Judge Wilson was still cleaning up his paperwork and I was still getting my table cleaned off and loading my briefcase when the jury chairman opened the doors and announced the jury's findings to the judge. How I wish you could have been here."

I thanked Steve once again for all he had done for me.

I was so impressed with the efforts of this marvelous litigator that I sent a letter to my insurance company's corporate offices thanking them for such sterling representation. I even told them the stories of how Steve had destroyed the "professional witness", and how he had "raised the dead" in my defense among other things.

I would never want to go through something like this ever again and I never had to. That week was one of the most interesting, though mentally draining weeks of my entire life.

The wannabees had wanted $750,000.00. They received zero!

Truth had prevailed.

EXIT – MY WAY

After the trial in Duluth, we finished the project in Mora, Minnesota, that year. My crew and I would go on, over the next nine years, to build nine more golf course construction projects bringing the total number of golf course construction projects during my career to 37.

During the majority of the time of my involvement in the industry, it was said that demand was such that each and every day, somewhere around the world, at least one new golf course would need to opened for play. And so, the golf course construction industry kept up the pace to meet this level of demand. Among the most popular projects being built near the very end of the twentieth century here in the United States were 18-hole golf courses surrounded by new housing developments. My crew and I built two such projects.

Around the time of the changing of the millennium, circumstances in the golf industry were changing as well. Golf, like other leisure time activities, is driven by and based on the leisure time enthusiasts "disposable income" or "discretionary spending". Regardless of the choice of leisure time activities, if that disposable income is diminished by outside factors which seemed to be the case at that time, demand for leisure time activities and the products and services that go along with these activities is diminished as well. This reduced demand was one of the driving factors in the downturn for new golf course construction at the time.

The weakened demand based on diminished disposable income caused a situation in which the golf market became flooded with golf courses that golfers no longer were playing. While it had been a problem in the past for golfers to get tee times at golf courses because of "heavy play", now it was golf courses desperately needing to fill sparse schedules with tee times. Many golfers simply couldn't afford to play the game any longer. This was a complete reversal of times passed. As a result, golf course revenues plummeted. When golf course revenues are down, so is the demand for new golf course construction.

Despite lower demand, I was able to negotiate a couple of projects to close out the twentieth century. Two of my last three projects were indicative of things to come and those things were not good. # 35 and # 36 were tough lessons.

Neither of these two projects were, in and of themselves, anything unusual in terms of golf course construction. All went well on both jobs. The problem had to do with the people I was dealing with. In both cases, I was dealing with predatory crooks who knew from the start of the project that they had no intention to pay the full agreed upon price as negotiated and signed for in contractual documents. In both cases, these projects were concluded in lawyer's offices. I was financially "beat up" badly in these settlements. The revenue *which I should have had* was substantially more than what the lawyers negotiated. What little I ended up with fell way short of the price for the work and everything else that these contracts had called for. Not only was there no profit, these two jobs had actually cost me money to complete. Project # 35 took me down. Another bad one back-to -back, # 36, took me to near insolvency. I was BROKE again.

This last time going broke, it wasn't weather or soil conditions, disputes, conflicting personality issues or anything other than dishonest people who never intended to pay as agreed upon from the get-go. Had it not been for these back-to-back predators, or if I'd have had a good job in between these two jobs, I could have "weathered the storm". But two crooks in a row with no intention of paying the agreed upon price were more than I could take financially. And then there were the lawyer fees on top of that.

In a way, this situation was my own fault. I claim that some of this is based on my background, the business environment I grew up in, and my business experiences of the past. Think back to earlier in this book when I told the story of my dad buying the sod field from the developer. At that meeting, which I was privileged at attend, I witnessed two businessmen who respected one another enough to know that a man's word was a man's word. It wasn't necessary to have a contract thick enough to resemble a Chicago telephone directory to do business. It was just two businessmen coming to an agreement and honoring one another enough to know they understood each other. This is the business environment I was brought up in. I'm not exactly sure when this type of straight forward, honest business dealing ended, but it happened. I was stuck in the past believing people at their word. Like my first time going broke, the tuition for the lesson was steep.

Now, like my father before me, I had gone BROKE twice as well! But like my father too, I was unbroken and ready to get back in the game. I reorganized again. I knew just what to do because I had previous experience.

After reorganizing, I was solicited to do another golf course construction project. My last, # 37, was my best ever job in terms of smoothness of operations, club cooperation, payment, profitability – everything. After completion of that project, I took a long hard look at what I was doing and the changed business environment I was now operating in. I made a major decision about my future.

For the first time in my life, I saw that there was really more to life than business. For the years since we had been married, I had abandoned my wife during the summer months to pursue my business interests. Living in this manner was selfish, greedy and an inconsiderate, stupid thing to do on my part. I'm lucky that she stayed with me through these years of marriage. I had disregarded her in my quest for materialistic goals which is in and of itself an insatiable obsession. I had been totally unfair to my wife while chasing the almighty dollar. I had to set new priorities. I had to be right with her.

Besides setting new priorities, I decided the risks in the business I loved were too great for a man of my age, my physical condition and my traditional business acumen. I was no longer willing to face the possibility of getting financially hurt as it seemed to me that the number of crooks in the business world was increasing exponentially. I knew I didn't do well nor did I understand this new business environment and all the savagery surrounding it. I had started over twice now and I figured that was about enough. Looking at my present situation in my business career and my personal life, I decided to quit business and make my exit. I sold off the machinery and vehicles I had acquired over this latest period of business. I exited the business world my way, on my terms and my conditions. I left the stage a winner like my father before me.

It was over.

PART VII – REFLECTIONS
Stories, Thoughts, Ideas, and Afterthoughts.

THE PORTLY GLADIATOR

As a businessman, how many times have I metaphorically envisioned myself in the role of a gladiator doing battle with a host of foes?

The scene; The Roman Coliseum, antiquity's greatest arena. It is here in this ancient sports complex that the question of life or death for the game's participants – the gladiators – was settled in bloody competition. Commonly, these contests, or "games" as they are called (how sadistic!) pit gladiators against exotic, ferocious wild beasts. Sometimes, for a different form of entertainment, gladiators do battle with gladiators. No matter, once participants are engaged in these "games", it is a fight to the death of one or the other contestants.

There I am on the floor of the arena doing battle. There is only one thing wrong with this scene though. It's my appearance.

I look ridiculous in my gladiator's outfit. I certainly don't fit the generally accepted norm of the classic gladiators made known to us in the epic films of yesteryear - of Kirk Douglas's portrayal of Spartacus, for example. A waddling gladiator, somehow, just doesn't fit the scene we have come to know thanks to the motion picture industry. Nevertheless, there I am, out on the floor of the arena struggling to stay alive, like my fellow gladiators.

Despite the ever-present danger, my non-gladiator-like appearance and my girth, I have been successful in the arena over the years. The fact of the odds stacked against me notwithstanding, I have prevailed again and again. My strength and my experience have carried the day.

On occasion, I have even won accolades for my skills from the high and mighty. I have defeated some of the best within gladiator circles. I have continually won the contests against the savage beasts. Though I may not have always totally defeated the beasts or gladiator foes, I have held them at bay until I won by decision. Remarkably, I have lived to tell this.

The arena has been good to me and I have become a respected gladiator. I have found great pleasure, pride and a sense of accomplishment doing battle in the arena. The gladiator's life has suited me well.

Then comes that terrible day I will never forget. The day one of the beasts blind-sided me – knocked me down – ruined me. The beast feasted on my flesh. I was so wrecked at the end of that battle, little remained of my former self. At the end of the fight, I had to deal with the fact that I could no longer be a gladiator. Just the thought that I could no longer do that which I had so loved to do was sickening to me. Being a gladiator was what my life had always been about. But now, after this horrendous battle, there I was – a broken, shattered remnant of the gladiator I had once been.

The really tough part about no longer being in the arena is that many of my friends and acquaintances were either gladiators or had something to do with the games. Now that I am no longer a member of that select brotherhood, I feel hopelessly lost and abandoned.

Because of my history and background, I just could not stay away from the games. It would be fair to say that I had, over the years, become addicted to the action of the games. Pathetically, I try to remain a part of the games though I have no place being there. I attend now, but rather than a participant. I'm just another spectator in the bleachers. I am no longer in the arena per se – a participant in the action – the action I was once so proud to be a part of. This is really hard for someone who had been so involved in the games in the past.

Some of my old gladiator friends see me up in the bleachers and wave to me once in awhile when they can. Some even come over to the wall to speak to me briefly before doing battle. It feels great just to talk to these guys again. It is wonderful to be remembered and shown some degree of respect for the gladiator I once was. Some remember, others do not or will not. Some purposely ignore me. GOD! That is tough.

The metaphor ends. Now, back to the reality of the business arena.

Think for a moment about problems faced day after day by people in the business world (the arena). Perhaps your business has had problems with employees, creditors, banks, insurance companies, government agencies, government bureaucrat's stupidity, sales, production, weather conditions, equipment failures and on and on. It would be a discovery moment to meet that business person who has never had problems in business.

The truth is, there is nobody in business who has never had problems. Being a problem solver goes hand-in-hand with being in business. Confronting problems, fighting through tough situations and overcoming obstacles is actually the essence business. It's not so much *dealing* with the problems you know you will encounter as *how* you deal with problems you are sure to encounter.

This is the environment we self-employed businesspeople deal in. As such, we must acknowledge that problems will exist in business and we had better prepare to do battle with these problems we encounter in our chosen business arenas every business day. Like the gladiators of antiquity, business people can never let their guard down. We must always be ready to face and overcome challenges if we are to survive in the arena.

Now that I'm no longer in the action on the floor of the arena but rather, have the spectator's perspective, it's funny what you notice *watching* the action rather than *being a part* of the action. This non-involved observation forces one to question the reasonableness of some of the games you've been involved in in the past.

From this new vantage point, the games and the opponents can be seen in an entirely different light. It is only by being *completely removed from the action* that we can clearly see exactly how risky and dangerous much of the action and many of the competitors truly are. From up here in the bleachers, given this new perspective, you begin to ask yourself why you ever participated in some of those games. Only now can we understand. Those of us who are former participants were so busy doing battle just to survive that we were unable to honestly and objectively view the games for what they really are– dangerous, high-risk endeavors. The truth is, you can't really see the games for what they are when you are busy fighting off the lions and tigers or gladiators. How very sad it is that one must be completely removed from the action to see what is actually happening in the arena, but how very true this is.

If you'd be willing to take some advice from an old portly gladiator, come on up here in the stands and sit with me. Take a break from the action and just observe what is going on in the arena. See if the games you play really make sense.

Have a seat.

WHAT ONCE WAS…

Should you ever go broke, and take it from a guy who has been there twice, the first thing to remember is that I would highly recommend avoiding it. But should you ever go broke, you are in for a learning experience about the realities of business the likes of which you've never ever even thought possible.

I'm just going to share some observations, some quick, hard truths about how your life will be severely altered if you ever have to endure going broke or suffer a major business setback. There are four things you must keep in mind at all times once you have suffered such a setback. They are;

1. Many of your old contacts in the business community whom you have dealt with on a friendly basis in the past were also your creditors whom you owe money but cannot pay at present. Most likely the only contact you will have with these business associates is demand letters and threats from their attorneys.

2. Your financial troubles are no secret in the business community. This negative information moves through the business community like an out-of-control virus. There is no hiding and there is no use attempting to do so.

3. To your former associates, it is as though you have become a carrier of the Black Plague. You will be avoided. You will be isolated from people you formerly associated with. Business people, especially, like to associate with winners and you are presently *not* a winner in any sense of the word.

4. When you really need help and information, your business associates and acquaintances, are no longer available to you. You need to seek out others in your chosen field of endeavor whom you know who have taken a setback or two. Not only could they help you with information you may seek regarding day-to-day business operation, they may share their thoughts, ideas and suggestions about the position you are presently trying to get away from. These people know better than to be haughty and arrogant with you because they too have had the "blocks knocked out from under them" in their past. If nothing else, they will listen to you and empathize with you and that is sometimes all you really need.

I've never known nor experienced absolute starvation-level poverty. However, going broke provided me with an opportunity to understand, in a way, oppression from the viewpoint of the oppressed. The main point to understand is that demoralized people are reduced to dealing with others from a position of total weakness. It is impossible to negotiate from a position of weakness. This powerlessness places one in the position of accepting that which is offered or going without. Having few, if any options, and no power causes an individual to fall into a hollow feeling of hopelessness which is directly associated with abject poverty. Poverty equates to limited choices while wealth affords those of means with many. I can now understand the downtrodden being taken advantage of and having no choice but to accept outcomes, however terrible, when in this miserable, impoverished predicament.

Prior to going broke, everything you had considered normal is totally changed, altered, different. What once was, is no more.

TURNED DOWN FOR LOAN?

Have you ever been turned down for a loan at the bank?

Congratulations!

You now have a wonderful, new opportunity.

But let me first share…

I remember the day well. I tried to impress upon the loan officer (not my man previously mentioned) that I had negotiated a good job and the profitability I'd built into the price was terrific. I showed him the numbers. I explained that I just needed a limited amount of capital to make a few payrolls and meet some expenses early on in the job. After those initial expenses were met, I'd pay off the working capital loan and everything would be handled on a cash flow basis – no problem.

As is the habit of bankers, they want to look at your last year's financial statements.

"Yes, the year before had *not* gone well," I admitted, "But last year has nothing to do with this year".

The response was (get this), "No, we can't *help you*." I was turned down flat – end of story. This was the first time I'd been turned down for a working capital loan.

Just a side note: I've always got a kick out of that banker's phrase - "help you". Let's see here, if he were really going to help me, I'm sure he would be happy to just let me use the money gratis. But it seems to me, as I recall, Mr. Banker, that you always want to charge me interest on that borrowed money. I recall paying a hell of a lot of interest over all the years I was being "helped". Just a little phony, perhaps?

Alright, so, I've been turned down at my bank. Well, it's not the only bank in town. I checked with other area lenders and get this deal going after all. Only problem is that the other lenders are also bankers who want to look at last year's financial statements.

 I continued to make appointments with bankers all over town and it was the same story. "We'd really like to "help you out", but based on your last year's financials, we can't "help" you." This was rejection on a vast scale. Over and over again, it was rejection. Going through all this is just another way to be made to feel low.

Based on these repeated rejections, I began once again, to question my worth, my business savvy, my aptitude for business. I became depressed. It was so clear to me. The numbers I shared with these loan officers showed a great profit margin. Surly they could see this. How could they turn me down for a small loan? I just couldn't make this make sense.

In my depressed mood, I couldn't think of a way to get this project underway. We, the golf course committee and I, had not yet signed anything and I hadn't showed my golf course customers my numbers. I just wanted to "get my ducks in a row" before making my presentation to the club. I sought the working capital loan because I wanted to be prepared to do the job. It would really look stupid if I had a contract in hand but was unable to perform on that contract because I was short of funds to get the job started.

I began to think of ways to make things work in my favor. I would need to consider something unconventional – a new approach. I would need to scrap the idea of "now that's how business is done" thing from my past.

I was no longer depressed as my mind was now occupied with finding a creative way to finance the startup of the job. At long last I discovered several things I had really never put to a lot of thought to in the past. It went like this…

1. The customer wants me to build a golf course for them.
2. I know exactly how to do just that and they will pay me to do it.
3. Why should I borrow money to do work for my customer?
4. The customer can make a substantial enough down-payment that *the customer will actually finance their project* from the get-go.

This is exactly how I solved my dilemma. I worded the contract in such a way that the down-payment was enough to cover my initial expenses and more. In so doing, the customer paid for their own project. I never had to borrow a dime on this project or any of my future projects. I didn't need the bank anymore. Besides everything else, seeking a substantial down-payment from the customer let me know that they truly had their finances in order before we even started the job. Why hadn't I thought of this before? Why had I been so shy about asking for a larger down-payment? Was it because of the "that's how business is done" thinking of past practices?

The way this turned out, what had been an obstacle to my doing business turned out to be nothing more than some character building and an opportunity to take a look at my past practices which needed revision anyway. In fact, the manner in which I was doing business in the past, I was paying interest on borrowed money wherein I was actually financing the project for the customer. How foolish! All of the loan officers who had turned me down for a loan had actually done me a huge favor by making me realize how backward the old way of doing business really was. Later on, I was genuinely grateful to those guys. They had forced me to get creative – to think!

When I began this, I said that if you'd ever been turned down for a loan, congratulations! Being turned down for a loan engages your thinking machine. That machine has just been turned on. You've been given a great opportunity. If you've been turned down, and if you are passionate about your business and want to continue doing what you love to do, you will need to take a look at what you are doing and how you're doing it. You too will need to become creative, innovative. As is often said these days, you will need to "think outside the box".

Just remember, there is a way through every tough encounter, every obstacle placed in your path. To find that way, well, that's up to you.

Start thinking.

WHIRLING

Those of us who have chosen to be self employed have done so for a variety of reasons, one of which is the dynamics of business. We enjoy variation – the movement – of the business world and the markets we serve. We survive or fail in this perpetual motion environment called free, private enterprise because we have chosen this rather turbulent lifestyle over that of a guaranteed daily routine. Reflecting back on my career, I find free enterprise to be either a whirlwind or a whirlpool.

The whirlwind is the fun ride. Always up, always increasing – constant gain and growth. Continuously an upward spiral, it seems as though this will never end. As the growth cycle continues, each turn produces higher and higher levels of achievement. In turn, this leads to greater and more wide-ranging goals. A business in the whirlwind mode results in financial ecstasy. Some people engaged in private enterprise are privileged spend their entire career in such a whirlwind. These are the fortunate few who never experience anything other than higher and higher levels of success, prosperity and wealth. Some of us enjoy the whirlwind ride for a while but not forever.

For some of us, the whirlwind stops. Our ride is over. Our business stagnates. Just remember, when we elected to be independent business people, we knew that business is dynamic. It is not a given proposition. So, then the question becomes, are we capable of catching another ride on the whirlwind? If you don't catch another whirlwind, you could be headed for a whirlpool.

Down you go! Small problems beget bigger problems which, in turn, beget yet bigger problems. Once caught up in a whirlpool, this downward cycle seems unending. The powerful currents of the whirlpool drag you deeper and deeper into the abys. A whirlpool ride is financial exasperation.

How many whirlwind ride candidates missed their opportunity because they couldn't read and understand the signals around them of the changing times within their market? How many lacked the guts to invest when the moment was right? How many were unwilling to take a chance at all? And then consider, how many whirlpool sufferers kept on struggling beyond good reason – continued beyond the point of no return?

Can you read the signs in your business environment? Do you get "that feeling" which allows you to tell the difference between a whirlwind opportunity and a whirlpool disaster?

I know I can do that now, but, then, I've had plenty of experience. The only problem I have with gaining this knowledge – tuition was hell to pay!

REALLY, "RED"?

Without a doubt, the greatest, most worthwhile, most useful class I ever had during my four years of college was one in the School of Business. This class alone has had so many practical applications for me in the real world of business. This class was all about salesmanship.

We were taught sales techniques by some of the greatest salesmen and/or motivational speakers in the country via film. The lessons by these powerful speakers impacted me greatly. They remain vivid in my memory today although decades have passed since the classroom. I have kept the notes taken in that class all those years ago and I used to refer to them for a little "tune-up" to "brush-up" on closing techniques for important deals.

One of those motivational speaker films was made by one of the winningest coaches in professional basketball, Mr. Arnold Jacob "Red" Auerbach, Head Coach of The Boston Celtics. The great coach naturally ties winning on the basketball court to winning in life, winning sales contracts and winning in business. Well, I'm not certain that a game played by seven-foot-tall multi-millionaires who can place a round object through a round hoop has a real-life tie-in to the world of business and sales, but, well, OK, if you say so, Red.

In his film, Red ties the entire sports-life-sales-business winning analogy together with this statement; **"SHOW ME A GOOD LOSER AND I'LL SHOW YOU A LOSER!"** Auerbach's point, of course, is to always win and never accept loss (a failure to win) with anything less than total disgust. It' always WIN! WIN! WIN! How many times have Red's immortal words echoed in my thoughts?

I understand Red's point about always wanting to win. Who doesn't? I can't think of a coach, an athlete or a businessperson who approaches a game or life or even this insignificant thing we call capitalism with anything in mind other than to win. Given the fact that I have gone broke twice, no doubt, Red's words certainly fit me. Or do they?

Going broke may well be the ultimate loss. At least, going broke certainly fits the criterion of being a loser. I'm convinced Red would argue that a basketball game gone bad is definitely a worse fate than merely going broke. He has his priorities and I have mine. The funny thing about our differing perspectives is that Coach Auerbach doesn't care that I went broke and I could care less about his basketball games. At least we have our indifferences to one-another's careers in common.

But is it at all possible that basketball really isn't related to business at all? Could this win, win, win, thing be a bit unrealistic?

GOD! HOW I HATE SPORTS ANALOGIES!

One of the big differences between the basketball game and the world of business is that I have total control over the final buzzer and the coach does not. When the buzzer sounds in the basketball game, that game is over, finished. The win or loss is final. The businessperson, on the other hand, gets to sound the final buzzer in their game only when they chose to do so. Nobody other than the entrepreneur decides when they are finished. Business losses are final only as long as they are allowed it to be!

While the seven-foot millionaires whine over such an earth-ending event as the loss of a basketball game, any loss a businessperson may suffer is nothing other than an opportunity to learn and grow and move on to play the game again. The businessperson is a loser only when willing to accept the loss as final. Therefore, any loss suffered by a businessperson has no permanency to it if that businessperson is not willing to accept defeat. The businessperson has a choice whereas the coach does not. Entrepreneurs can rethink, reorganize and regroup to get back in the game if they want. The coach can't.

Looking back on it now in a perverse sort of way, I'm rather glad I suffered my losses. This would really bug Red. You know why? After losing, the winning is all the sweeter, the victories all the more splendid. Had I not experienced loss I could never have known the thrill of winning again.

Furthermore, had I not admitted that I lost – had I continued to struggle or deny my downfall – the loss would have become even worse. Being a good loser, I admitted I was in trouble and needed to sell down my assets "my way" rather than letting the bank do it their way. I ended up with something rather than nothing. Being a good loser allowed me to rise up again to play the game one more time rather than "being on the bench" (to use the language of athletics) forever.

There's one other thing I would have liked to have shared with Red had I had the chance after watching his film. In sales, it is said, salesmanship starts with the word "NO!" I'd say that's baloney, too. When a good salesperson hears "NO!", they *know when no means "NO!"*. Experienced salespeople understand "NO!" and are smart enough to move on to the next opportunity. Their attitude has to be that the bigger, better deal is just around the corner. Therefore, the professional salesperson wins by admitting defeat. They go to the next prospective customer rather than wasting time with those who are uninterested in the product or service offered by the sales professional.

So, I must admit that I *do not* believe in the theoretical ties between the game of basketball and the game of life or salesmanship or business no matter how dynamic the motivational the speaker. I'm a good loser. My experience tells me that my attitude and my acceptance of my loss allows me to better deal with loss and then to move on to be a WINNER!

That's how the real-world works. Really, Red!

THOSE GUYS

You don't have to be a businessperson to know that they are out there.

What I'm talking about are crooks, thieves, robbers, dishonest people. And, it seems, these sorts of people are becoming more prevalent.

Whether you want to or not, you will encounter those who, if given the choice of doing something the right way vs the wrong way or the legal vs the illegal way, they will purposefully choose the wrong way or the illegal way. The hard truth is, that's "how they are wired". I've known them, worked for them and with them. Probably so have you.

Many of these characters are fun and entertaining to converse with. They are interesting to be around and it's okay to be around them. You just need to avoid doing business with them at all costs. You can't win. You will lose every time.

Signing a contract with folks of this nature is not unlike British Prime Minister Neville Chamberlain signing a peace agreement with the dictator Adolph Hitler. Like Hitler, these characters have no intention of honoring any agreement. Agreements, contracts or letters of intention are meaningless jokes to individuals such as these. They view others as nothing more than suckers, stool pigeons, or just another victim to add to their already long list of those whom they have cheated or been less than honest with. It's all about them and the "*them*" doesn't incude you. It is their habit to conclude what may have been understood by you to be a solid agreement or a contract is a fantasy or a joke in their lawyer's office.

Unfortunately, we have to be somewhat cynical about doing business with people nowadays. Learn to "read" people. Check out potential customers as thoroughly as possible before engaging in any business dealings. Don't be afraid to demand a substantial down-payment. Doing so, you needn't stay awake nights worrying about collecting later.

Remember, *those guys* are out there.

GUARANTEED

I'll bet you know many people, like I do, who want everything in their lives to be definite, beyond question, unalterable, rock solid, guaranteed. I've known folks who can tell you exactly the number of working days left before they can retire several years ahead of the actual date. They can rest assured that their health care insurance, their savings accounts, their pensions and investments are all secure. Their lives are pre-planned down to the most minute detail. I'm sure this affords them a sense of comfort, security and protection. Good for them.

Although I find this to be strange, given my background, I respect them for their organizational abilities and good life planning skills. Different from my circumstances, but understandable, maybe even admirable. These people are OK with me.

However, there exists a sub-group within this group though which bother me to no end. These are the arrogant elitists among the life planning group. They will tell you that they will never take a chance and feel that those who do are stupid. They are so much smarter than those damn fools who take risks. To this group I'd like to point out that it is these risk-taking damn fools who;

- build our infrastructure
- build and operate our transportation system
- manufacture our clothing and footwear
- build the vehicles that move us

- build the homes we live in
- provide the insurance which guards us from peril.
- provides the travel and leisure time opportunities we enjoy
- manufacture all of our consumer goods
- grow and deliver all of the food we eat

Instead of acting so haughtily towards risk-takers, perhaps this group should consider the facts. It is in fact true that these damn fools provide all of the above to the citizens of this nation and they do so without any guarantees whatsoever.

I guarantee it.

THE TRABANT

Looking back, I am delighted to live in a country where free, private enterprise thrives. I'm delighted that I had the opportunity to take risks and enjoy the rewards, and yes, even to go broke. These are all elements in the continuum of free, private, independent business.

I'm saddened that there are proponents of communism and socialism at work in this haven of free, private enterprise, The United States of America, nowadays. These communists and socialists are making headway with far too many of America's youth.

Unfortunately, these youngsters don't know any better because they don't know the history of failures of both socialism and communism. They need to learn of this history before they are sucked in by this utopian philosophy which just doesn't work for the betterment of people in the real world. Capitalism does work. Both communism and capitalism have sound "track records". History proves this.

I would bet that today, if you asked young people what a corporation is, they would respond, "evil" or "corrupt" or "crooked" or, well, anything but the truth which is simply that a corporation is a business model in which people gather together to do that which they can't do individually. It is free enterprise.

Communism, on the other hand, is based on ownership or control of commodities. This "worker's paradise", in Karl Marx's philosophy is based solely on materialism. In Marx's words; communism is all about the "ownership of the means of production" by the proletariat - the term he uses for working people. (Interesting that this idea comes from a man who never worked a day in his life.) Like all material things, this philosophy based on material things can never and will never last.

Democracy and the free enterprise system, on the other hand, is based on the non-materialistic will of a free people which is without monetary value, and therefore priceless.

I have advice for youngsters who are toying with the idea that communism is a better form of government and a superior method of providing the most and the best goods and services to citizens of any nation. Do a Google search for "Trabant".

The Trabant is an automobile that was manufactured in Communist East Berlin, Germany, basically from the end of World War II until the end of the Cold War when the Berlin Wall came down. Under communism, if you wanted an automobile in the communist Democratic People's Republic of East Germany, it was the Trabant and only the Trabant. Consumers had no choice since there were no other makes or models to select from. It was either a Trabant or nothing. There was always a long waiting period to get a Trabant since the workers assembling these things had no incentive concerning productivity. This poorly designed, ugly, inefficient, uncomfortable, loud, polluting, shoddily built, stupid little car was produced for nearly 40 years unchanged – without any improvements of any kind whatsoever. These vehicles were so bad that the body parts for these things were actually made from an industrial by-product or otherwise waste material. The "central planners" had a choice; either 1.) landfill this industrial waste or 2.) make auto body parts for this junky little car out of this stuff. They chose option 2. And that's how it was with the Trabant for the next 40 years.

During the same time period in which the Trabant was being built under communism, in the free market operating with capitalism through free enterprise in the United States of America, there were constant improvements in vehicle design. Improvements and innovation in vehicle design and safety came about because of competition. The individual endeavors of imaginative, creative, and inspired people who love to compete kept improving their products while Trabant improvements never happened.

Continual advancement. Always seeking the betterment of products. Improvements happen when free people get to make free choices.

With communism, there is no need for change or improvement anything since there is no competition involved. The Trabant is truly the "poster child" for everything concerning the so-called benefits of communism.

Our uniquely American free, private enterprise model is how things work best for humankind. Business happens here in the U.S.A. because there are individuals with the courage and the fortitude to "go it alone" and compete. The efforts of these free-spirited, risk-takers are what always has and always will maintain the United States of America as the great nation that it is. I'm proud to be counted among those who have "gone it alone.".

You can keep your communism, central planning and the Trabant itself which best represents the communist philosophy. I'll take free enterprise and the marvelous advancements for humankind developed through competition, capitalism and the free market.

The Trabant – poster child for socialism and communism

CONTRACTOR/PHILOSOPHER

After my first time going broke, in the depths of my depression, I was talking to anyone who would listen to my problems. I needed advice. There are no reference manuals, directories, or guide books to offer help to businesspeople in the predicament I was in. If only there were a "Broke for Dummies".

I spoke to any number of my associates and fellow contractors who had taken a financial fall. Many gave me some real sound advice. But one stands out above all others...

For this story, we'll call him Bob.

I pulled my pickup into Bob's yard. He was working inside of a sports van replacing the interior paneling. I got out of my truck and walked over to the van. He heard me approaching and got out of the vehicle. He took one look at me and said, "What's with the long face kid?"

I said, "Bob, I'm looking for answers and the answers I seek are really hard to find. I just don't know what to do."

"Why, what's up?", he asked.

We had known one-another for years and I felt comfortable sharing my problems with him. I told him the whole story - the job, how the weather had killed me, how I had to face the banker, selling off all of the equipment and how this was tearing me apart. When I ran out of sorrowful, pathetic things to say, Bob began;

"Well, you and I have known each-other for years as businessmen and contractors. We've done business together and we've competed against each-other. During the time we've known each-other, it has only been as businessmen. We know little or nothing of one-another as human beings. I know that you know that I went through what you a are presently experiencing. It's no fun but, you'll get through it. I know you can. But let me tell you a story."

"As businessmen, there's really no reason for you to know this about me but, I'm a good Irish Roman Catholic. That being said, my wife and I were really very good at making babies. We had five in a row – BING, BING, BING, BING, BING! My wife was raising those babies while I was building up my business."

"As you are well aware, there was a time, in this area, when I was quite a contractor. I was considered to be a "real player" back then. During those times when I was building up my business, all of the machinery dealer's salesmen and all of the truck dealer's salesmen would wine and dine me several times a week. It was nothing for me to be invited for a luncheon or dinner at the area's finer dining establishments three, four or five times a week. Or maybe it was just cocktails after work at a local tavern. There were always the free fishing trips or the free tickets to professional sporting events these salesmen and I would attend together. All of these guys treated me like I was really something special. These guys were my social "friends", in a business sense, and we shared some really great times and had a lot of fun together."

"Of course, they did all of this wining and dining and sharing the good times with me knowing that if I had a good business year, I would be a buyer of the equipment they were selling. Then came my fall. One bad job took me down. I went broke."

"Suddenly, my "friends" didn't know me. Now that's a sad story, isn't it?"

I said, "It sure is Bob."

"NO", Bob said, "That's not a sad story. The sad story is that my five children didn't know me either!"

WOW!

NUTS AND BOLTS

At 3 years old on one of Dad's International Harvester TD 18 bulldozers.

For as long as I can remember, I've been around machinery, trucks and equipment. As an infant, my dad placed me on one of his large bulldozers to have my picture taken. I remember that as a youngster, without exception, all of my toys were small replicas of trucks, tractors and earthmoving machinery used by contractors. In my early youth, I was definitely being influenced, if not brainwashed, by my surroundings.

In my adolescent years, the pattern continued. During that time in my life when I was too small to operate equipment but too big to play with toys, I would go with my father to visit project sites and watch with limitless fascination as the equipment moved and shaped the earth. My acquired taste for this was insatiable.

Diesel exhaust from these machines was not an odor to me, it was an aroma to be savored, a fragrance to be relished. Each diesel engine manufacturer's exhaust had its own unique bouquet and I could smell the difference. The roaring, clanging and clattering of the different pieces of equipment was not so much noise to me, rather it was a symphony, a great concert, a harmony of sounds all orchestrated by giant yellow instruments. I loved these things.

In my early teens, I became more curious, as boys of that age seem to do, about the mechanics of the machines and what makes them work and why. My father saw to it that I had an opportunity to learn, first hand, how machines work, why they work the way they do and how these mechanical beasts are put together. After school, I would work in the shop with the mechanics who were repairing the machines. My job ranged from washing parts to fetching tools and other no-skill jobs. Nevertheless, I did learn how machines work, how machines break, how to make repairs and what holds machines and the parts that make them up together.

I continued to love these things.

My desire to acquire more and more machinery gave me my passion for doing business. My grandfather's passion had been well drilling, my fathers was making person-to-person sales. This desire of mine to add more and better equipment and larger and newer vehicles to my fleet was what pushed me to take bigger risks. The bigger rewards from these bigger gambles (that was the theory) would generate larger volumes of capital with which to add to the fleet.

While the driving force for me was machinery, for many, the desire for more and more wealth is what really excites them about business. For others, it's raising one's social standing. The great motivator for others could be fame, or power, or lust, or just plain greed. Whatever form of overindulgence drives us, each of us has that certain something which motivates us to do what we do.

I would encourage you, if you've never done so, to think about what it is that drives you. Knowing and understanding your motive will give you a better understanding of yourself. This better understanding of yourself will serve as a solid foundation upon which to build, or if necessary, to rebuild whatever sort of career or business or life journey you may choose.

After my business unraveled and I personally became unglued, I had to re-evaluate my life. No longer was machinery acquisition or business involvement the priorities they once had been. After much thought, I knew I needed new priorities. It was clear that my materialism was not at all healthy.

I discarded materialism and took a different path. At that juncture, new and important questions came into focus now such as;

- What is it that really counts in life?
- How do I develop higher priorities than those of my past?
- How have my personal goals of the past been unfair to others?
- How do I do the most that I can to help others?
- How will I be remembered by others?

After all the years in business, I was forced by circumstances to take a long hard look at these questions. What a great blessing this opportunity for a re-evaluation of my life has been.

Of course, the old machinery theme, was still the basis of my thought pattern. Having been devastated businesswise, I viewed my business and my personal life as though I was a broken-down bulldozer scattered all over the repair shop floor. I was dismantled down to the smallest castings, the littlest gears, the bushings, the bearings – all of the tiny parts that comprise the great machines.

That's when the nuts-and-bolts idea struck me. Machines, no matter the size, when reduced to their most basic, fundamental components are fastened and held together with rather simple devices – nuts and bolts. I knew that if I was to put my life back together again not only as a businessman, but more importantly, as a human being, I needed to find some nuts and bolts.

I thought to myself, now that my life had fallen apart, it would be the right time for me to find these figurative nuts and bolts that would put me back together and then hold my life together as a person and as a businessman. So, this rather simplistic thinking took me to the point of asking myself what are or what should be the really important elements of my life. It was this nuts-and-bolts idea which held the answers I was looking for. What are these nuts and bolts that could put and hold my life together?

The head of a bolt and the exterior of a nut, those surfaces which receive the pressure from the wrench when tightening or loosening these fastening devices, are hexagonal – six-sided. This six-sided idea or the six points on a hexagon fit in well with what I found really mattered to me.

After spending a lot of time and giving this matter a lot of consideration, my findings are as follows. The things that really matter to me are:

1. Faith
2. Family
3. Friends
4. Reputation and/or Integrity
5. Personal Health
6. A dream

When I surround myself with this hexagon, these six points of priorities, all else is reduced to nothing more than commodities. Of the six points, not one has a monetary value. I am certain of the value of these six priceless assets in my life. When my list of true assets no longer contains material things and stuff, the loss of material things and stuff becomes completely immaterial. Fame, fortune, social standing and all the things and stuff society would have us believe makes a difference, really makes little difference at all if we can reject materialism.

Be it machinery, money, favorable social standing, buildings, cars, stocks, bonds – whatever you have been led to believe is of value - if a price can be established for that item, it is nothing other than a commodity which can be bought or sold. Changes in commodity ownership take place every day. Therefore, the ownership of any commodity is as tentative as is success in business. One day you have it – the next day you don't.

I have chosen not to, therefore, measure my intrinsic worth either as a businessman or a human being in terms of things or stuff gathered around me whose ownership or value can be changed. I now believe I have value that cannot be bought or sold. I will no longer allow my self-value, my self-worth as a living, breathing human being be based on material things in the manner I did in the past.

Should I find that any of the six points have taken on a monetary value, it will be time for me to dispose of that part for it is no longer an asset to me. I will not allow any of the six points to become a commodity.

If a family member or a friend stands by me only so long as I have monetary value to them, I could no longer consider such a person to be an asset to me. If my faith, my religion and my church are only with me so long as I provide monetary support to the organization, it should be viewed as a business and the type of business I no longer choose to do business with. True family, true friends, true faith can never and will never sink to this level of materialistic bastardization. Therefore, family, faith and friends are priceless to me.

My reputation is mine alone. No one else has made it, whatever it is. How my reputation is viewed by the community and my fellow business associates is completely my responsibility. I believe I cannot escape the reputation I have made for myself – either good or bad. If I possess a good reputation, it was earned over time and I must protect it because it is like a non-material, highly valued jewel. My reputation, my integrity cannot be bought or sold. It cannot even be improved by spending money to enhance it. It is priceless.

Personal health is also priceless. What good is anything if you are not in good enough health to enjoy the world around you. Try to fix a price on your good health. You can't.

Take away my dreams and I have no reason to get up each morning. My dreams, my hopes, my aspirations are all based on the premise that tomorrow I will improve my lot in life and improve the world around me for the betterment of those who are my responsibility and/or those whom I hold dear. Without a dream to work towards, to drive me on, I cannot find a life's goal.

Priceless treasures, these six points that I found when thinking about nuts and bolts.

These are the nuts and bolts that hold my life together.

A FEW RANDOM THOUGHTS

Never "bet it all" on one hand of cards, one roll of the dice or one huge project.

- Pride can be a very expensive burden.
- Devote a few moments every day pure thought, just for the fun of it.
- Experts abound – after the fact.
- No matter what happens to you, enjoy life. This is the best life you're going to have.
- Know what your real priorities are and remember to keep them in the right order.
- Debt, like a chainsaw, is a vert useful tool. Use either one carelessly and you will get hurt.
- Nobody should try to fail, but it's a crime to fail to try.
- Setbacks give us the opportunity to see if we chose the best path to take on our life's journey.
- If you choose to make excuses, you will deny yourself the opportunity to make a difference. If you choose to make a difference, you will deny yourself the time to make excuses.
- It really doesn't take much "gray matter" to deal in the "gray area". Make solid decisions. Make definitive choices. Don't be a coward.

- If you want to find out who your real friends are - go broke.
- You can't move ahead staring in the rear-view mirror. Behind you is the past. Learn from it, but then look and move forward.
- If you can put a price on anything, it has no true value. If you can't put a price on it, it is indeed priceless.
- Keep your good word. It may cost you in the short run, but the long-term dividends are marvelous.
- Never forget your past. Offer to help others who find themselves where you have once been.
- Friends who are true are few.
- Only people who try have the opportunity to fail. Please include me that list of those who try. It is only those whose names appear on this list who make a difference in the world.
- Understand that a loss can actually be a win in disguise.
- If there really wasn't going to be a tomorrow, would you be happy with what you've done today?
- Is your work really worth it? Would you spend today at your job if you knew today was your last day of life?
- Failures are merely lessons in riddle form which need solving.
- If you've gone broke, you understand that you will remain broke only until you decide you don't want to be broke any longer.
- Seek the knowledge and experience of others who have gone down the path you are now traveling. Time spent listening to these individuals is a priceless treasure.
- "IF" can be a treacherous word. When followed by "only" or "I'd have" it gets dangerous. Quit dwelling on the past.
- Perseverance! A good word to always keep in mind.
- Have a plan for your business as well as your life goals.

- Are you living to work or working to live? If you are living to work, you may want to step back and take a look at your priorities.
- Decide whether you want to manage or work. If you want to work, buy a lunch bucket and go to work. If you want to be in business, your job is to manage your business and that, not working, will be your full-time job.
- Financial liquidity is a far better asset than tangible assets.
- Shop around and choose the right banker for you and your business. Then work to build a two-way relationship based on mutual trust and respect.
- It is far more noble to *reach down* to help others than to *look down* on the less fortunate. Who knows? You may find yourself back down at the bottom one day.
- I'm going to enjoy as much adventure, fun and laughter as possible. You know why? I'm going to be dead for a hell of a long time!

AFTERTHOUGHTS

My business career was halted for a while because I quit. Rather than looking for opportunities, it was easier to dwell in self-denial, self-pity and admit defeat. It will always be easier to be a quitter – a loser. When I quit trying, when I gave up, I really was a loser in every sense of the word. Trying or quitting – that was the choice only I could make.

Perhaps, a businessperson should take a mid-life sabbatical. Getting away from business for a time is a great way to sort out your life. My break from business was forced on me by my financial demise so that was less than ideal. Stepping away for a time, although not necessarily by choice, was a healthy thing for me to do. It allowed me to discover that financial liquidity is more important than the acquisition of mechanical assets. Growth in terms of additional asset acquisition at the cost of liquidity is stupidity.

For a time, I was a risk-junkie. I can jokingly refer to this condition of mine as a genetic mutation based on my family history. Let me assure you that risk-taking can be an addictive opiate. Since my downfall, I have voluntarily surrendered myself for de-tox.

As a risk-junkie, I never developed a business plan. I had never developed a life plan either. Not having a plan to go by is foolishness. You are "a sheet blowing in the wind" – directionless. Not only does one need a plan for your business and your life, but you need to write those plans down on paper. Only with a written plan can you determine success or failure because you have established points of reference. Set goals and then review these goals often to determine how your business activity is performing and how your life's journey is progressing based on these goals you have set. Only then can you ascertain how you are doing.

Only those of us who have taken a fall know the best way to get back up. Those of us who have been on the junkpile of human wreckage understand which nuts and bolts to use to reassemble our shattered lives. We who have been forced to admit our failure know that there is no permanence to failure unless we allow that permanence to be the case.

We have an advantage in whatever we should choose to do with the rest of our life over those who have never known failure. We no longer fear failure. We know that we can win despite it. We have the courage to try again even if that next attempt should result in another failure. We see opportunities and we have the guts take advantage of these opportunities while others are timid and afraid. We have learned from our setbacks. The cost of these lessons has been overwhelming, but, that's life! Pay the price. Learn the lessons. Move on.

If I had it to do all over again, would I choose to make the same life journey? Would I take that roller-coaster ride called free, private enterprise even if faced with a setback or two?

YOU BET I WOULD!

Even knowing the risks and dangers involved, would I trade the freedom, adventure and excitement of being a self-employed entrepreneur for the security of a routine, monotonous, boring, mundane 9 to5 job?

HELL NO!

I'D RATHER GO BROKE!

www.ingramcontent.com/pod-product-compliance
Lightning Source LLC
LaVergne TN
LVHW091539060526
838200LV00036B/665